Confused Spice

Mathis Bailey

Copyright © 2016 Mathis Bailey
All rights reserved.

ISBN: 1535124423
ISBN 13: 9781535124423

1

Pierre

"**N**ot enough butter!" shouted the French instructor from across the room.

It was my first day of French cooking class. Learning how to make flaky dough with loads of butter was worth my 350 bucks. I love butter ... and so do my hips and ass. I must have tried every Paula Deen recipe under the sun. She was my Julia Child, that is until she romanticized the whole back in the "good ole' days plantation style" wedding thing. What was she thinking? Oh Paula. Anyway, I couldn't wait to get home so I could practice the emulsifying techniques to make this silky chocolate ganache, which was the next week's lesson.

As the bus rattled down Midland road I looked down at my class notes and read the ingredients: "eggs, milk, cocoa powder and butter." I made a mental note to pick up more butter. I shoved the grease-stained loose-leaf papers back into my notebook and stared out of the window, reflecting how many strawberry tarts I'd shoved into my mouth. Guilt suddenly hung over me like an ominous dark cloud. That was a gazillion hours on the treadmill for sure. The husky Quebecois accent of the instructor suddenly came to mind: "Too much cornstarch, too much sugar, NOT ENOUGH BUTTER! ... measure, measure, measure!!!" I must say I struggled in measuring out all those damn ingredients on the topsy-turvy scale. But I managed and came out on top. I even managed to garner some praise from my fellow classmates, who wore crisp white aprons and puffy-looking chef hats. I thought this day couldn't get any better until I arrived at my apartment building later that evening.

Nothing prepared me for what I saw, something far more delicious than the chocolate ganache recipe tucked away in my shoulder bag. He was tall, dark, and handsome. Cliché? Yes! But by god he fit the mold — everything I like in a guy. His skin glistened like rich mahogany wood. His hair was freshly lined in a close-faded cut. He had deep, dark eyes with eyelashes that would make you melt like cold butter on a hot stove. He stepped onto the elevator behind me, and we stood in silence. I could smell his natural sweet body scent as if he was just coming from a light workout. His warm-up shorts hung on his lean, muscular frame like an NBA player. He glanced my way, catching my stare. I quickly looked away, pretending to gaze mindlessly up at the red digital numbers counting up. It took every ounce of my self-control not to look back at him. Yet I could feel his eyes on me. *Come on! Say something witty, Pierre.* The elevator jolted and knocked me out of my reverie. It started to ascend, and I noticed he hadn't pressed the button for his floor. Should I say something? Before I could, he spoke.

CONFUSED SPICE

"Hey, my name is Jay," he said, flashing a gorgeous smile. "I always see you in the gym on the treadmill. You sure can run for a long time, yo. How long have you been running like that?"

"For a few months," I muttered, thinking, *He's seen me before? How could I have possibly not noticed this beautiful stud?*

"I wish I could run like that, but my diet has been horrible lately. I need to get back into shape." I examined his body and saw the faint definition of his toned chest underneath his white V-neck T-shirt.

"You look well in shape to me," I said.

"Ha! Thanks, man. I try." Modest ... or was he just being cocky? Either way, it fit him well, like a tailored Italian suit. He looked roughly twenty-five, give or take. Not much younger than me. The elevator stopped on the eighth floor, and a plump white man stepped on, parting us like the Red Sea. Jay's beautiful body scent now was being masked by a box of Chinese takeout. Unable to think of anything else to say, I looked back at the numbers on the elevator. My stop was eighteen. Another ten to go. *Great! A countdown!* Now I was racing against the clock. I was completely tongue-tied. The elevator halted at eighteen, and the doors slid open. I smiled meekly at Jay as I stepped out onto my floor. I inwardly flung expletives at myself for not thinking fast on my feet. I knew I was going to regret not making a move. There was a possibility that I would never see this beautiful man again. I turned toward my apartment in a gloomy state until I heard a silky voice come over my shoulder. "Ain't that someth'n, yo. I guess we're neighbors!"

3

2

Vijay

"What do you mean the woman in Pakistan doesn't matter? She is seeking refuge in this country from her abusive husband. Yes, I know she is, but..."

I heard my mother's voice booming on the other side of door. I knew she was again on one of her business calls. I knocked, and when I didn't get an answer, I pushed it open. She didn't look up from the mountain of papers on her massive oak desk. I strode over to the big reddish brown leather chair in the corner and plopped into it. She lifted her eyes over the rim of her reading glasses and put up a finger that said "give-me-a-minute." I sighed heavily, containing my frustration. I looked around at all her prestigious degrees aligned meticulously on the cherry oak wall, from the University of Toronto and Ryerson University in Law and English.

CONFUSED SPICE

"Yes! Fine! I will see if that will fly in court!" She slammed down the phone. "What can I do for you, Vijay? I hope you aren't into any sort of trouble. My time is valuable."

"No, I'm not. And stop treating me as if I am one your clients. Talk to me like your son."

"Vijay, just tell me what you want. I do not have time for this."

"You seem not to have time for anything except for your new family." I had raised my voice.

"Is everything okay in here?" asked my stepfather, poking his head around the door, always butting in on our disputes. I don't have anything against the guy. Frank is a cool dude. He is one of those hippie white guys that enjoys the outdoors and eats nothing but locally grown Ontario organic products.

"Everything is fine, Frank," my mother said as she massaged the sides of her head while Frank shot me a suspicious look and then disappeared. "Vijay, just tell me what I can do for you? Do you need money?"

"No, I didn't come here for your fuckin' money."

"Vijay! If you are going to use that kind of language in my house, I will have to ask you to leave. So stop wasting my time and tell me what you want. I have a very important phone conference beginning in a few minutes ... so make it quick."

"I would like for you to come see my new place."

"And where is this place?"

"It's in Scarborough. It's a beautiful..."

"Scarborough! Are you dealing drugs there?"

I drew in a deep breath. "No, I got a job. And like I said before, that was a mistake I shouldn't have made. That life is behind me now."

"Vijay, I do not have the time to come down to see your new place. I am swamped with work."

5

"What's new?"

"If it weren't for me working, you wouldn't be in that new place you're in right now. Now if you don't mind I have to get on a call"

"Fuck this shit. I'm leaving anyway." I flipped the papers on her desk for effect.

"Get OUT!" she screamed as I existed her office.

⌐ ⌐

"Come on man ... you can do it. Give me four more," said my fitness trainer as I was bench-pressing a shit-load of weights.

He held one side of the handles for support while veins in my arms bulged out as I tried to give two more but dropped the weight in its cradle, which made a loud clank sound, metal hitting against metal. I was done for today. I took a swig from my water bottle and strolled into the locker room. I stripped naked and took a hot shower. I rubbed the Ivory soap over my stomach and sex, creating a foamy lather. After rinsing off, I patted down my body with a white towel and sprayed on some cologne. I took a pair of jeans out of the maple-colored locker and put them on and then threw on a white V-neck. Before I left GoodLife Fitness, I gave my trainer a fist pound and strolled out the door.

I pulled up to my new apartment and parked in an empty spot in the visiting section. I was too tired to park on the third floor in underground parking and wait for the stupid elevator. I grabbed my Nike duffle bag from the back seat and headed inside the building. I nodded "what's up" to the concierge as I strolled toward the elevator. As I placed in my key in the door, the guy

CONFUSED SPICE

that I met yesterday walked off the elevator right after me. He paused for a second and smiled. I smiled back, and before he placed his key in his door, I invited him in.

3

Pierre

I shoved my keys back into my pants pocket and strode over across the hall to Jay's apartment. He said he had a spectacular view of the city and that I must check it out. *Can this really be happening?* I wondered whether he was hitting on me. Um, no way. I convinced myself he was being nice and neighborly. But the thing is, I never had a straight guy be so nice to me before, let alone a good-looking one. He had to know I'm hetero-challenged.

I sauntered into his apartment, where stacks of dirty dishes lay in the sink. He dropped his black Nike gym bag at the door and began to clear the kitchen countertop that was littered with junk mail and shopping receipts. He looked at me, embarrassed.

"Excuse the mess, homie, I haven't had time to clean today. Let me take out the trash and I'll be back to give you a grand

CONFUSED SPICE

tour," he said as he lifted the overflowing garbage from the bin, still looking slightly chagrined.

Even though the garbage was overflowing, the place still smelled immaculate, like toasted coconut and warm apple cinnamon. He came back and closed the door behind him.

"Are you thirsty?"

"No, I'm fine. Thank you."

"Hey! I didn't catch your name?" he asked, opening up the refrigerator and pouring himself a cup of lemonade.

"Pierre."

"Yo, that's a tight name."

"Thanks, Jay."

"Vijay is my real name, but people call me Jay for short."

Indian? Interesting. For some reason I thought he was black with his fresh line-up and smooth, dark complexion.

He sauntered over to the window with his dollar-store plastic green cup in hand and drew the cream-colored blinds, which rattled as they separated. "Look at this, man. Isn't it great?" he said, taking in a deep breath and a long sip of his drink. I strode over and took in the panoramic view that over looked a sea of houses and the hazy skyline of Lake Ontario, with the CN Tower in its midst. This view was way better than my own, which overlooked a busy highway and a few crummy factories.

"Yeah this is awesome, Jay. I didn't know this apartment could get a million-dollar view all the way in Scarborough. How much do you pay a month? If you don't mind me asking."

"I don't mind; fifteen hun."

"Whoa! Really?"

"Yeah — I know it's a lot, but I had always wanted a view like this, and now I have it."

9

I thought to ask what he did for a living but figured it would be overstepping my bounds. I looked around the apartment, sizing up the space, and noticed it was two times bigger than mine. He told me he had two bedrooms plus two baths. I looked over to my right and could tell the couch was a hand-me-down. My guess was it came from his grandmother or aunt. It was floral and had dingy marks. A phone book substituted for a leg. In front of it stood a glass coffee table strewn with colorful packages of condoms. Vijay's eyes followed the direction, and he quickly covered the condoms with a stack of *Men Health's* magazines.

"Like I said homie ... excuse the mess," he said, now standing up straight like a soldier in a roll call.

"That's okay," I said, smiling meekly and averting my eyes to the barren white walls.

"I had a hot brown girl over last night."

"Oh, okay," I said plainly, hoping he wouldn't go into further details and then turn around and ask me about my sexual escapades with the ladies. All of sudden I was disappointed that he was straight.

"I see you're wearing a chef's coat; do you cook?" I looked down at my attire and suddenly felt embarrassed and unattractive. I brushed at a strawberry jam stain that was staring me in the face, taunting me about how many strawberry tarts I ate in class.

"Yes, but I'm not a chef." The lines on his forehead furrowed in confusion. "I'm taking a French cooking class just for a hobby. I enjoy cooking and baking, you see."

"Word? So ... that what's up. I would love to learn how to cook. It gets tiring eating takeout food day in and day out. It is so unhealthy."

"Yeah, you're right."

CONFUSED SPICE

"So, would you be interested in teaching a brotha how to cook? I mean, I'll pay you, of course."

"Paying me won't be necessary. I'd be happy to teach you."

"Cool." He smiled. "Well, in that case, groceries are on me." He palmed his phone in hand and keyed in my number. We agreed on a cooking day, which would be every Thursday at eight in the evening. He escorted me to the door and gave me an Obama knuckle-pound before we parted.

I slid the key into my door and saw the red light on the answer machine blinking. I tossed the keys on the kitchen counter and thought about Jay. My god, he was handsome. I pressed the button on the answering machine: "Hey there GONE WITH THE WIND, this is your best friend, Demarcus, the one and only. I'm coming up there for New Year's. So make sure you make a bitch feel welcome. I booked my ticket, and I'll email and text you the details tonight. Talk to you later," and another beep followed. "Hey baby, I hope you got my texts. I miss you, give me a call."

All my wonderful thoughts about Jay and I schmoozing on an intimate night, feeding each other strawberries, had instantly vanished like a Twinkie in a fat kid's hand. I dug into my pants and pulled out my cell. I pondered making the call. I scrolled down my list of numbers until I saw Dre's. I took a pause, thinking over what to do. I was still pissed off about what happened between me and Dre. Just the thought made me furious all over again. I figured I still needed more time to think things through. I tossed the cell on the couch and strode into the bathroom to take a long, hot shower with Vijay suddenly appearing back into my mind.

4

Vijay

"Vijay, what is this I hear? You received another speeding ticket?"

There I go upsetting her again. But I don't give a flying fuck! I held the phone far from my ear until she relaxed. It gave me pleasure making her upset. Why should I be the only one in pain? This was my umpteenth traffic ticket, and had it not been for my mother knowing some esteemed colleagues, my driver's license would've been revoked a long time ago, and I probably would've been thrown in jail on top of it. It doesn't hurt to have a mother who is one of the most powerful lawyers in Toronto. All my mother's colleagues remembered me as that cute kid who would run up and down City Hall whenever she brought me to work. Now they knew me as that guy who was always in trouble. I plopped on the couch in my living room.

"Yeah, I got another ticket. Who told you?"

"Don't worry about who told me. You know people in my profession tell me everything. Vijay, you cannot keep going around with this reckless behavior. I don't want anything to happen to you."

"I think it's a little bit too late to behave like a mother to me. I don't live under your roof anymore. Remember?" I said sarcastically; she had thrown me out of the house when I was twenty, not for my back-talking but for bringing drugs into her perfect suburban home in Markham. I was out one day hanging with friends in Brampton when she found marijuana in my pants pocket while sorting laundry, so she claimed. I think she was snooping, sticking her nose in places where it didn't belong. When I got home, she yelled and screamed and told me to get the fuck out. She never liked any of my friends, many of whom were Sri Lankan and Jamaican. She thought they all were low-life hooligans. I felt my mom never really forgave me for bringing drugs into her home. When Frank found out about it, he agreed with my mother that I needed to get out and that they couldn't afford to have my little sister stumble upon it. I had been on my own ever since.

For a few years, I lived with my stepfather's sister, Paula, who lived over on Sheppard Avenue. I still sold weed and hung out all sorts of hours. Paula was never home due to her hectic work schedule as a flight attendant traveling all over the world. But whenever she was on vacation from work, she would spend a lot of time at home and that's when my life became restricted once again. She had set a certain time for me to be in the house. Fuck that. I saved up enough money to get my own place, a nice little sweet spot off Ellesmere and Kennedy, where an elderly Russian lady was renting out rooms in her white bungalow. It was a humble-looking house with manicured bushes and planted flowers. It had three bedrooms and two baths and a finished basement. The rent was hella cheap. There were two other roommates in the house when I moved in. One was a thirty-four-year-old Nigerian guy, a big fellow with broad shoulders who stayed to himself. The other was a lean thirty-year-old white guy I never spoke to until one morning I saw him in the kitchen pouring himself some herbal oolong tea. His blonde hair was dreaded and pulled back with an elastic rubber band. He wore a dingy white shirt and khaki shorts with big side pockets.

As he made his way to the backyard with his tea, I followed suit with my bowl of Cinnamon Toast Crunch in hand to see what this dude was up to. As I watched from the doorway, he sat on a tree stump with his legs folded. I was amazed how motionless this homie was. He slowly closed his eyes and stayed in that ridiculous position for a good amount of time. Minutes later, he rose and did some weird stretches. He looked my way and motioned me over. The sun was high in the sky and stung my eyes as I made my way over. The strong scent of wildflowers and other plants made me want to sneeze, but I held it in. He kept his eyes on me as I moved toward him. I stopped midway, keeping a comfortable distance.

"I see you are interested in my activities," he said, picking his cup of tea off the grass and taking a sip.

"Yeah, man, how did you do that?"

"Do what?" he asked, taking another sip and looking amused by my question.

"You know, having your legs behind your head and such."

"Oh, that took years of practice."

"Okay, that's what's up."

"I beg your pardon?" he said, looking confused.

"Whatever you were doing, it looked pretty cool."

CONFUSED SPICE

"It's good for the body and mind. You should try it some-time," he said, brushing the dirt from the balls of his pale feet.

"Does it have a name?"

"It's a form of meditation. It helps clear the mind of any neg-ativity and brings your inner thoughts into the present moment."

"I think I should try it one day"

"Yes. You should. It will help you become one with your true self." He took another sip of his tea. "What's your name?"

"Vijay. Yours?"

"Donovan, but you can call me Don," he said, picking a book up off the grass.

"What you have there?"

"*The Monk Who Sold his Ferrari.*" Cool title, I thought. I wouldn't mind owning a Ferrari of my own. A goal I want to achieve. All I had to do was sell enough of these treez.

"Do you mind if I take a look at that?" I asked

"Sure."

I placed my bowl of cereal on the wooden patio table and grabbed the book from Donovan's hand. I flipped through the worn pages. I read a few passages from it and became interested. "Can I read it after you're finished?"

"Sure. I got all I could get from it. I guess you can say my cup is half full." I looked at homeboy confused as fuck. Don laughed and said, "I'm done with it. I hope it brings you as much peace as it brought to me. Consider it a gift. If you come across any pas-sage that is vague, be sure to come to me. I wouldn't mind going over it with you."

"Thanks, bruh. I really appreciate it," I said, turning around and walking back into the house, reading the book as he watched me from behind with a strange smirk as if he just built a space-ship to save the world.

15

As I was in my room, furnished only with a convertible mattress and an electric tea maker, I sat there and read the book that Don had given me. It opened my eyes about who I was as a person. All this time I was trying to live up to something that my mother was trying to make me be, which drove me to seek validation in all the wrong areas in my life. All this time I had to look inside myself. This little book answered questions that I had always pondered: *Who am I? What is my purpose? How do I become a better person?* I read all day, losing myself within its pages. When I finally looked up, it was night. I forgot all about dropping off this bag of weed.

I saw my phone light up a couple times. It probably was a druggy or a thotty Scarborough hood rat that needed to be fucked nice and proper. I reached for my Galaxy, and it was the latter, a girl who I fucked on the regular. Her name was Priya. A cute, light-skinned Indian chick I met on the street. We weren't in any serious relationship; she was just someone I sexed up from time to time. I could sense she wanted more out of the relationship though. Lately she's been asking me questions like why didn't I respond to her texts. Why didn't I buy her something for Valentine's Day? How come I didn't take her out to the movies or to a nice restaurant? This chick was becoming a little too much. For lack of a better word, a nuisance, like my mother would say. Perhaps I needed a break from pussy. But not tonight. I was horny as fuck. I phoned her and made it happen.

The next morning, as I escorted Priya out the side door, I ran into the landlady. She wore a cross expression. She was working in her garden, wearing white gloves and a big hat to shield her from the hot summer sun. She looked around to make sure the neighbors weren't watching and made her way toward us in a big huff. She looked Priya up and down with a glare of disapproval, which propelled the girl to make haste to her purple Smart car.

CONFUSED SPICE

Once she left, the old prune told me there were no girls allowed in her house. *What the hell? Am I twelve?*

I managed to sell enough weed within a couple months to move the fuck out.

I found a little piece of heaven that suited my taste and vowed to myself that my life would be different from that moment on.

"Do you hear me, Vijay!" I snapped back to reality as I heard my mother's voice booming on the phone. "Vijay, I am done bailing you out. Do you hear me? This is the last time. The last! This has to end."

"Whatever," I said nonchalantly.

"Oh really. Would you like to pay off these tickets that are towering on my desk?" I was silent. I knew it would take me a lifetime to pay off these tickets. However, I knew my mother would easily have them expunged from my record with one quick phone call.

"Now, Vijay, I want you to straighten up. Quit all this foolishness and apply yourself to something meaningful."

"Like what … a journalist?"

"No. Something more stable than that. I want you to be all you can be."

"No. You want me to be what you want me to be."

"Vijay, if you only knew how fortunate you are."

"Not this talk again." She usually lectured me about her clients living in Third World countries, deprived of identity, money, and education.

"And when are you going to get married? The boy down the street that you used to play with, what's his name?"

"Rajeev Kapoor."

"Yes, him. He's married and finished university. And what are you doing? Nothing."

I used to play with Rajeev when I was a kid. We were best friends. We would run around and play hide-and-seek. He was one of those brown guys that did everything his parents goaded him to do, like excel in every subject, become a doctor or a computer engineer, and when all was said and done, get married to a nice Indian girl from a respectable family. That shit wasn't me at all. Over the years we eventually grew apart.

"Vijay! Are you there?"

"Yes, your Grace."

"Don't you get smart with me. You could learn from him."

"No! He could learn a thing or two from me," I said, but she didn't hear. Her line clicked, and she placed me on hold. I knew it was a business call. She clicked back over.

"I have to take this. Remember what I said, Vijay. No-more-tickets." And then the phone went silent. No I-love-yous or goodbyes. This was our relationship, day in and day out.

I rose and popped in Tupac's "Dear Momma" and then went into the kitchen to pour me some OJ. I thought about texting Pierre. I wondered what he was up to and if he would be down to cook tonight. When I reached for my phone, it lit up. I thought it was Pierre. I picked it up off the coffee table with a smile and looked at the text, it was from Tameka. This black sistah I'd had a thing for ever since grade school. She needed some extra cash to pay for her paint supplies for art school. I texted her back, saying not to worry, that I would be more than happy to lend her the money. It just meant that I would've to hustle to sell more treez, then after that I'd quit this way of life.

I was still trying to get inside those panties, you see. I hated the fact that she only saw me as nothing more than a friend. I texted her back, asking if she'd like to come over to see my new place. She texted back: *"Not tonight."* Fuck her! Why did I keep

CONFUSED SPICE

stressing over these bitches? I tossed the phone on the coffee table and plopped onto this fucked-up sofa. What was my life coming to? I wasn't going anywhere. All of a sudden I felt miserable. Alone. My phone vibrated on the table. I let it dance a bit before picking it back up. Perhaps she was going to let me hit it tonight after all. It was my mother. She was probably calling back just to nag. I tossed the phone on the other side of the sofa and rose to fix something to eat. I opened up the fridge, and a carton of day old milk and a jug of OJ stared me in the face. I looked in the cabinet, where there were ramen noodles, chicken flavored. Before I ripped open the orange package, I flipped to the back and read the nutritional value: Fiber 0, Sodium 830, Saturated Fat 3.5. There was no way I was putting this into my body. My eating habits had to change. I threw it into the garbage and poured a glass of orange juice. I thought about ordering takeout and then nixed the idea. I had a better thought. Pierre.

5

Pierre

I felt my cell phone vibrate near my crotch … *Oooh, it's Jay.* He sent me a text: *Yo Pieeerre, what you sayin? Are you down to cook tonight?*

Is he serious? He *actually wants to hang out with* me? *At his place? Alone? At night?* But it even wasn't Thursday yet. However, I did tell him to call me anytime he wanted to cook. The fact that he thought of me sent chills through my body. I found Vijay so irresistibly good-looking and sexy. *But is he straight, gay, or bi?* I texted him back, saying I would be home in forty-five minutes. I was still at work, and I wished this woman would hurry up and buy something. I could not wait to get out of this boring-ass department store. The blonde woman was fluttering from one rack to the next, wearing an indecisive expression, with her pink lips pursed as if she was emulating Paris Hilton.

CONFUSED SPICE

"Pardon me, sir, do you have this in a size 6?" she said, holding a white poodle in one arm and a Chanel dress in the other.

"Um ... miss, just to let you know the store will be closing within a couple of minutes."

"Yes, I know, but I must have this dress. It is totally my style. You look like you have a keen eye for fashion. You tell me what you think." She held the dress up against her Anna Nicole frame. I looked down at my wristwatch and read five minutes past nine. *Shit!* "It looks wonderful, ma'am, but unfortunately it is the last size." So... I lied. I knew more had come in this morning as I was doing inventory. But I was not going to rummage through those boxes for a size she would return the next day. This bitch needed to go. Fast.

"Oh dear! That's a shame ... isn't that right;, Princess?" she cooed to her poodle, which was wagging its tail furiously. "I sure do love this dress. Do you have anything similar to this?"

"No. I'm afraid we do not." She pursed her pink lips as her poodle barked in her defense. "I will suggest you come back in a couple of days. That is when we will have more in stock."

"I actually need it for tomorrow night for this fabulous dinner party that I was invited to," she said, tapping her stiletto on the hard, white, polished marble floor.

This woman was getting on my last nerve. I looked down at my watch again. It was a quarter past nine. *Double shit.* I'd told Vijay I would meet him at ten, and it took me an hour to get home. Why did I have to work all the way downtown at Bloor and Yonge? *Damn you, commute!* "I'm sorry, ma'am, but we are closing now."

The woman butterflied to another clothing rack as if she hadn't heard me. At this point I was inches away from calling security. However, I wasn't sure it would be a good idea. I had to be cautious with customers like her. She could be a politician's wife for all I knew, since this was the high-end part of town. She could possibly have the juice to shut this place down. I could see it now: "Ottawa mayor's wife thrown out of Saks Fifth Avenue." The door beeped, and it woke me from my reverie. I looked around, and the corpulent woman and her mutt were gone. *Yes! Let's close up this bad boy.*

I felt my phone vibrate once again. "Where you at, man?" *Shit!* It was Jay.

I consulted my watch. It was a quarter past ten. The train was finally pulling into McCowan station. I got up and stood by the door, waiting to dash out like a speeding bullet, but all of a sudden the train stopped over the bridge. *FUUUCK! What's the hold up now?* I looked out the window. There was another train still loading passengers inside the station. *Great! Just my luck.* I consulted my watch again. Eleven o'clock was quickly approaching. I knew Vijay was falling asleep and would cancel the whole thing. I needed to get off this bloody train, even if I had to do some MacGyver moves. An elderly white woman clutching her purse looked at me suspiciously as I paced back and forth like a caged tiger, waiting for the train to come back to life. The train jerked and started to move again. Once the doors slid open I dashed out like a Jamaican sprinter, flying down the escalator, bumping into people who were moving at a slower pace. The cold stung my cheeks as I stepped out into the night air. I thought about catching the bus, but then I took another look at my watch and thought to walk it. My place was only fifteen minutes on foot, even less if I jog. I walked and jogged with my hands tucked deep into my

CONFUSED SPICE

jacket. I suddenly felt the vibration of my cell. *Oh lord, its Jay sending me another text. This time to cancel for sure.* I stopped and reluctantly reached down into my pants pocket to pull out the phone. "I want to see you tonight." *Double fuck!* It was De'Andre. My cheating fiancé. I ignored the message and shoved the phone back into my pocket. I trucked on and arrived at my building. I rushed pass the concierge and beamed toward the elevator. I pressed my floor button feverishly.

I arrived on my floor and did not hear anything coming from Vijay's apartment. I pressed an ear against his door and heard the TV running. *Yes! Hope is still alive.* I brought my shoulder bag to the front, which was strapped across my chest. I pulled out my favorite cologne by Paco Rabanne and sprayed a light amount on my neck. I lightly knocked on the door and waited a moment. There was no answer. *Noooo.* He must have fallen asleep and left the TV on. Panic rose in my chest like a tsunami rushing onto a calm shore. I knocked again, but this time more pronounced. Nothing.

I strode to my apartment in despair. Once inside, I threw my keys onto the kitchen counter and switched on the lights. My stomach begun to rumble, and I checked the fridge for any morsel of food. I grabbed a piece of old fort cheese and chewed it like a horse eating hay. I took off my clothes and flung them on a lazy boy chair near the window. I plopped onto the couch wearing nothing but my cute yellow and blue American Eagles undies that De'Andre bought me.

My phone lit up and danced around on the kitchen counter like it was possessed by an unknown entity. *Could it be him?* Hope rose within me like the walking dead. *My bed is cold*, it read. I looked at the number and recognized who it was from. "Um yeah, tell that to your other boo," I said to myself. I

23

ignored the message and tossed the phone onto the other side of the couch. Despair sat back in like a welcome visitor. As I rose and went into the kitchen to pour a glass of red wine, my phone went off again. Maybe I was being too hard on him. Everyone deserves a second chance. Besides, my bed was cold too. I took a sip of wine, strode over to the sofa, picked up the phone, and read, *Come over.* My heart skipped a beat. It was Vijay.

His door was cracked open as I stepped out into the hall. I knocked and heard a faint voice tell me to come in. I sauntered into his apartment, where scents of mango and orange blossoms assaulted my senses. *My God, his place smells so good.* I heard ruffling coming from his bedroom.

"Yo Pierre, make yourself comfortable. I'll only be a sec."

"I thought you were asleep. I came over and…"

"Nah, I would never sleep on you bruh. I was in the shower, but I heard you knock and figured it was you. Besides, you promised you would cook me something nice, which I been anticipating all day. I couldn't sleep on that yo." I could imagine him flashing that million-dollar smile as he spoke. He came out the bedroom wearing black warm-up shorts and a crisp white V-neck T-shirt with his feet adorned in black Nike ankle socks. He was so close to me that I could smell the Irish Spring soap on his chestnut skin. I saw small beads of water trickling down the crack of his toned chest.

"Can I get you anything to drink, man?"

"Yes … please." I felt my mouth getting parched from all the sexiness he exuded. He opened the fridge, and I saw it was empty. "Where's the food, Jay? You remember I had texted you a list of things to pick up."

CONFUSED SPICE

"Oh, I thought it would be fun for us to go to the market together." He had a mischievous grin on his beautiful face while he was pouring my glass of lemonade.

"Jay! Do you have any idea what time it is? It's almost twelve o'clock at night. Are you sure you even want to do this so late?"

"Yeah bruh, I don't mind. I'm always up this late, and besides, my blood is still pumping from my late night workout at the gym. So are you down?"

"This is some tomfoolery, but yeah, I'm down."

"Great," he said, handing me my glass of lemonade with a quizzical expression.

"What?"

"That word you used, tom something."

"Oh ... tomfoolery? It means, craziness, very silly."

"Look at you with all these fancy words. You sound really intelligent yo."

"Thanks." I laughed lightly. *Wow, this guy is so good for my self-esteem.*

"Let me just throw on my shoes and we can get going."

"Hold up! You just wearing what you have on? Do you have any idea how cold it is outside? It's almost below freezing," I said, staring at him in his basketball shorts as he slid on his black Jordans.

"It's okay. I'm Canadian. I'm used to it."

"So you know, I don't have a car. How will we..."

"I have a car. Let's go," he said, throwing on his black trench coat without breaking stride.

He drove a black 2002 Acura sitting on silver chrome rims with tinted windows. It certainly matched his bad-boy persona. I hopped in, and he took off out the parking garage like a bat out of hell. He made twists and turns on every street corner,

25

avoiding all red lights and yield signs at all cost. So this was how it felt to be with a naughty straight boy. My adrenaline was racing. My heart had no words to express this crazy endless night. He popped in Jay Z and pressed harder on the accelerator as the music boomed through the speakers. A wicked grin spread across his handsome mahogany face as he sped faster. "Jay, the light is turning ree..." He flew past it, flashing me a catlike smile. We arrived at Metro grocery store in one piece.

"Man, Pierre, you need to learn how to relax when you're with me."

"You drive like a madman."

He let out a sinister laugh, tossing his head back, and strutted into the store as if he owned it.

⏤ ⏜

"My boy Pierre is teaching me how to cook," he said excitedly while pulling the groceries out of the plastic bags.

"Are you kidding me, Jay? Do you really want me to teach you, or you want me to do all the work while you watch TV?" His carefree personality made it easy for me to joke with him in a facetious way. It certainly felt like we known each other longer than a few days.

"No bruh, I am serious. I want to learn."

Wow, a straight, handsome guy wants to help me cook at one o'clock in the morning. This is surreal. Is he bi? I wondered.

"So what do you want me to do first?" he asked, looking confused, like a lost child in a department store.

"Cut those onions sitting on the chopping board." He grabbed a small knife and started chopping an onion at a snail's pace. Once the oil in the saucepan had started to crackle on the

CONFUSED SPICE

stove, I added fresh chopped ginger and garlic. As it started to sizzle, I reduced the heat on low. I opened the cabinet where he kept cups and plates. I closed it and opened another. *Ah-ha!* I rummaged through the bottles of McCormick spices and saw only pepper, salt, oregano, basil, and thyme. All the essentials for baked chicken and spaghetti.

"Um ... can you stir this while I grab something from my apartment? I won't be long." He nodded, and I jogged across the hall to my apartment. I plucked a few spices from the cabinet and raced back over. As I sauntered back in, there was something sexy about seeing his six-foot frame hovering over the small saucepan. As we went back to our designated positions, I noticed Jay staring at me surreptitiously as I placed a few spices in the pan. *Oh my goodness, is he checking me out? This cannot be happening.* Good thing I wore my H&M skinny jeans.

"What?" I asked, turning around away from the stove.

"Um ... nothing ... well..."

"Yes."

"It's just that ... I don't like spicy food," he professed, poking out his bottom lip.

"Oh ... coriander isn't spicy. If you don't believe me, have a smell." He sauntered over to me with his dark eyes peering into mine, emanating a delicious hesitance. I raised the bottle underneath his beautiful sculpted nose. He leaned forward, closing his long-lashed eyes and taking a deep, lingering whiff. He no longer smelled of fresh soap but of raw onions.

"So?" I asked.

"It smells good, man. It has a lemony scent." I nodded and smiled at his keen senses. "But are you sure it's not spicy?"

"I am sure; besides, you should be able to take spice. Aren't you Indian?"

MATHIS BAILEY

He laughed.

"What's so funny?"

"Yes, I'm Indian, but not the ethnicity you think."

"Huh?"

"I'm Guyanese."

"Guinan-what? Is that in Africa?"

"Guyanese, bruh. Don't tell me you don't know where it is. You're black!" I shot him an expression that said *what-is-that-supposed-to-mean?* He continued, "Aren't you from the West Indies?"

"No, I'm American."

"No way! You're American?"

"Yes. What's the big deal?"

"There aren't too many Americans I know that live here, that's all. I should've known you were from the States. You have a drawl in your voice."

"I do?"

"Yeah. It's almost sounds southern. Where are you from?"

"Detroit."

"No way! Not only you're American, but from Detroit. That's my favorite city, man." This little piece of information about myself seems to give me such credibility. Vijay's face lit up like a fat kid in a candy store everytime I revealed something new about myself. "Does that mean you know how to make soul food?"

I laughed. "How to make it? I was brought up on it."

"You know how to make sweet potato pie?"

"Of course."

"Yo, you must make that for me. I always wanted to try it. I've never had soul food before. I always hear about it on *The Game* on BET. Do you watch that show?"

"Sometimes."

28

CONFUSED SPICE

"Dude, I love that show. So what was your reason to coming to Canada?" he asked, placing half of the chopped onions into the hot saucepan and returning to chop the other half. I knew this question was going to come up sooner or later. I thought about telling him the truth.

"I came here to be closer to my lover," I said simply.

"Oh, she's Canadian?"

I paused and said, "Yes, but she is actually a he."

Silence filled the room.

"You're gay?"

"Yes, I am."

"Yo man, I'm not gay," he said, throwing up his hands, dropping the knife onto the chopping board like a burglar caught red-handed.

"That is fine, Jay, but I am, and if you have an issue with it, I will be more than happy to..."

"Nah, nah, that's not necessary. It's just that I have never had someone come out to me before," he said, resuming pensively chopping his onions. We returned to our duties in silence, dropping the subject. I sensed he had more to ask but didn't know where to begin.

Twenty minutes later, the food was ready, and we sat on his dilapidated couch and flicked on the TV. He flipped to *Jersey Shore* and then scooped a spoonful of food into his mouth. Watching him eat was pretty sexy. The way he had the plate close to his face made me wonder how good he was at foreplay. I stared at him, waiting for a verdict.

"This is good, man!"

"Thanks," I said, with a big smile.

"What do you call this again?"

29

"It's a chicken and black bean Cuban dish. I got the recipe from one of those *Men's Health* mags. They really have great recipes in them.

"Honestly, this is better than my mother's cooking. Keep cooking like this and I am going to have you move in here." *I wouldn't mind that at all,* I thought.

After the meal, Jay's eyes were becoming bloodshot. I could tell sleep was coming fast. Deep down, I was not ready to go. I was comfortable in his presence. However, I didn't want to overstay my welcome. He walked me to the door and propped an arm against it.

"So, soul food next week?"

"Sure, sounds like a plan."

"Alright, see you then. Goodnight, man."

"Goodnight, Jay."

6

Vijay

The next morning, I decided to meditate for the first time. I let out a wide yawn, sat beside my bed with my legs folded, and took in a long, deep breath. The room was silent. I tried to be still and calm, as demonstrated by the hippie who lived at my last place. I tried to remember his exact words: "Just be still and try not to think. Just be." I sat there for a few minutes and was bored as fuck. Before getting up off the floor, I did twenty pushups. I felt blood rush though my body after the last one. I felt awake.

I strolled into the living room and plopped on the sofa. I grabbed my phone to see if I had any missed messages from any hot girls. Zero messages. I tossed the phone on the coffee table and switched on the radio, and Drake's song "Over" came blaring through the speakers. I rocked my head to the beat as I made my way to the kitchen to pour myself a glass of orange juice. I looked over to the stove and noticed I'd left out the food that Pierre and I cooked last night. I picked at the spiced meat and placed the rest in the refrigerator. I went back to the sofa, switched on the TV, and flicked to BET. *The Game* was on. I licked my lips as I saw Wendy Robinson strut her fine ass across the screen in a tight skirt. She had a nice ass. An ass that I would definitely hit. I leaned forward, still licking my lips while taking another sip from my glass. I felt my sex becoming semi-erect.

Pierre suddenly came to mind. I wondered what he was doing. I wondered if he would be interested in coming over, just to chill or to cook. I couldn't remember the last time I had so much fun without a dumb thot being involved. And Pierre being gay didn't bother me at all — as long he kept that gay shit to himself. I looked up at the clock above the TV. It was 11:00 a.m. It was still morning. He was probably at work. I sent him a text anyway, asking if he wanted to cook tonight. I held the cell in my hand, waiting on his reply. Nothing. I guessed he was busy at work. I placed the phone on the coffee table, picked up my glass of orange juice, and finished it. I put the empty glass in the sink and switched off the radio.

I strode back to the sofa and picked up a new issue of *Men's Health* with Obama on the front cover. He had on a crisp white shirt and a black tie, perched on a desk. This guy had so much swagger, I thought. I thumbed through a few pages and corner-folded the ones with interesting, healthy recipes that I might cook with Pierre. After I finished looking through it, I picked up a book on the coffee table with Dalai Lama on the cover. I wanted to give this Buddhism thing a shot. Perhaps this faith would help me with my fucked-up life. I cracked open the tattered book I'd checked out from the library. But before I could read the first sentence, my phone lit up. It was Pierre. He was down for tonight.

7

Pierre

Yo Pierre, What's you say'n? Down to cook tonight?
These tantalizing words had a way of making my heart beat rapidly. Lately Jay had been sending me texts just to hang out at his place. We didn't even cook on our scheduled days; every day seemed to be our cooking session. He enjoyed going to the supermarket at night, so that's what we'd been doing before our cooking sessions.

It was a quarter past ten. I sprayed on Paco Rabanne and placed on a fitted V-neck red sweater. I looked myself over in my bedroom mirror and liked what I saw. Before I could put on my shoes, I heard a rap at the door. I peered through the peephole. It was Vijay. I opened the door and he had on dark jeans, a black V-neck T-shirt, and a cream-colored trench coat with the collar flipped up.

MATHIS BAILEY

"Are you ready?" he asked, slipping halfway inside my apartment.

"Yeah, just need to put on my shoes." I reached for my red Converse near the door. As I was slipping them on, Vijay swept his eyes around my apartment in a judgmental manner, with his bottom lip fixed in a shrewd way. I knew he was thinking how small it was compared to his palace. I suddenly realized this was Jay's first time in my apartment, and it felt weird. I hurried up and laced up my shoes before he asked for a grand tour. I grabbed my keys, and we were out the door.

As he was driving down Progress Avenue, he turned up the music and played Jay Z's song "Hard Knock Life." A few minutes later, I noticed the gas light came on. I pointed to it, and he pulled up into a Petro-Canada station. Before he got out, he turned to me and asked if I wanted anything, with his beautiful dark eyes pressing into mine. I shook my head and thought how chivalrous this guy was. This wasn't the first time this had happened. One evening on our way back home from the market, he stopped at a Tim Hortons. I didn't want anything, so I stayed in the car. He came back with two coffees. With a bright smile he hands me a cup of hot coffee made the way I like it: one sugar, two creams, stirred, and with room. Gestures like that made my heart melt like ice cream in the Indian summer. He was so sweet. I just couldn't figure out why he didn't have a special lady in his life. Perhaps he was too unstable. Or perhaps he was picky, or bi-curious.

We arrived at Kennedy Commons and parked in front of the Metro supermarket. We strode along the produce section, where I bagged a couple of tomatoes, onions, and garlic while Jay grabbed a couple of apples and oranges for himself. An elderly black woman beside him was struggling to open up a plastic bag.

34

CONFUSED SPICE

Jay eyed the woman and noticed her hands trembling. My guess was she had Parkinson's disease. Jay ripped another plastic bag from the dispenser and opened it. He helped the woman pick a few firm apples and placed them in the bag for her. She thanked him and gave him a warm smile. This was a side of Jay I'd never seen before, and I found it irresistibly attractive. We headed toward the self-checkout, and I reached in my pocket for my wallet. Jay put up a hand and offered to pay. I really didn't have a budget with Jay; he allowed me to pick up anything I wanted. Whenever I refused his generosity, he would tell me he forgot to pick up something and ask me would I mind getting it for him, and by the time I returned, the groceries would be paid for.

Back in the car, Jay wore a sneaky smirk. *What does he have up his sleeve?* I wondered.

"Pierre. I just got this amazing idea."

"What is it?"

"Look." He waved his hand in front of him like an emperor showing off his kingdom.

"What?" I leaned forward, peering into the dark night.

"The parking lot ... it's empty. Are you up for a little fun?"

"It depends what kind of fun you are talking about," I said with a little lilt in my tone, forgetting the nature of our new relationship. He looked at me incredulously. And I simply said, "Sure."

He was beaming from ear to ear. He placed his foot to the metal and took off in swirling circles ... kicking up white smoke. My right shoulder was pressed against the door as we spun around menacingly. My adrenaline was racing. I had never done anything like this in my life; this was crazy. Certainly none of the guys I'd dated in the past were this adventurous. Vijay looked at me with delight and excitement, which I mirrored. He cranked

35

up the music, and Rihanna's song "Only Girl in the World" came blurring into my ears. It sent shock waves through my entire body, which shook my core. The song was saying everything I was feeling in that moment, right there, right then. I'd heard the song before and liked it, but tonight had brought out its true meaning. As the song hit its crescendo, he sped faster. I felt my tongue in my throat. Part of me wanted him to stop, but the other part wanted him to keep going. He powered down the windows and hooted and hollered in liberation. I smelt the smoke burning from the rubber on the pavement as the tires made screechy noises. He finally spun out of the looping circle and hopped on the 401 highway, high on life.

When we reached home, the rush of adrenaline had evaporated as quickly as air in space. We sat the groceries on the counter and started cooking. Vijay cleaned the clams as I chopped the tomatoes. He never knew clams had whiskers until I showed him the brownish strings on the sides.

Once the onions and garlic started to sizzle in the pan, we added the clams, the coconut milk, and white wine. Jay had never cooked with booze before, and this excited him. He was beaming from ear to ear as he poured Pinot Grigio into the saucepan. He said he felt like Bobby Flay and the fat dude that wears rubbery shoes. I assumed he was referring to Mario Batali, given that I had Jay watch a couple of his cooking shows one day on the Food Network. I went into the spice cabinet and took out some spices that were unfamiliar to Jay. They were mine that I had left over his place from our last cooking session. He stared at me with that suspicious look.

"What is that?"

"Chili powder and turmeric. I'll promise I won't make it spicy."

"Bruh, I don't know. I don't like the smell of that stuff."

CONFUSED SPICE

"Have you ever smelled turmeric?"

"No."

"Well, how do you know you don't like it?"

"Because I know what I like."

"Would you like to taste it or take a whiff, just to be sure?"

"No thanks, bruh."

I saw he was in his adamant mood. When he wasn't looking, I added a dash of each spice to the pot. When the garlic bread was done in the oven, we made our way to the battered couch with plates in hand. I waited for Vijay to take the first bite. He dipped his spoon into the reddish-orange broth and took a slurping sip.

"Pierre, my man, this is delicious!"

"Seriously?"

"Yeah. It has a really nice flavor. Hats off to the chef."

"I can't take all the credit. You helped, you know."

"Yeah ... yeah ... but you have that touch," he said, dunking a piece of crusty French garlic bread into the broth and speaking with his mouth full. "What spices did you put in this again?"

"It's my little secret."

"Come on..." he pleaded.

"Well ... you know the spices I pulled from your cabinet earlier." The slurping and clinking of the spoon against bowl came to a halt.

"Are you serious, bruh?"

I nodded with a bit of guilt. "I didn't add a lot."

"Well, it's surprisingly good. I normally I don't like it in my food, but this is proper."

"Turmeric and chili powder, are they common spices in Guyanese food?"

"They are, especially amongst Indians. But I wasn't brought up on spicy foods."

"Interesting."

"Yeah, all my brown friends would say the same thing. Every time I got invited to a friend's place for dinner, I would be the only one sitting at the table eating raita and ro tis. The only things that weren't ninja spicy."

After we finished eating, he had something to show me. He went to his bedroom and returned with a Mac laptop that must have cost well over a thousand bucks. This model wasn't even supposed to hit the market for a couple more months. I wondered how he got his hands on it so fast.

"How did you get that?" I said in a surprised tone.

"It was a gift from my mother," he said, sitting beside me with a winsome smile. "She knows someone who works at the Apple Store. A woman she helped out in a case."

"Okay ... that was nice of your mother to get you this."

"Yeah, she can be nice when she wants to."

"Jay, can I ask you something?"

"Yeah, sure, man."

"Do you think she gave you this to make up for all her wrongdoings?" Perhaps I was crossing my boundaries, but I had to say it. A couple days ago, Jay had shared with me how he and his mother were always fighting and had a somewhat estranged relationship.

"What do you mean?"

"Like not coming here to see your place. Perhaps she gave you this to keep you out of her hair."

"I don't know, man. I mean, she can be a bit bossy, but her heart is always in the right place."

"Well, how come you guys fight so much?"

"I don't know, it's the nature of our relationship." I felt there was something more Jay wasn't telling me.

CONFUSED SPICE

"Have you guys ever consulted a counselor? Or a psychiatrist?"

"Yeah, once."

"And?"

"The doc blamed everything on me and thought I was suffering from depression, and prescribed me some fucking pills."

"What kind of pills?"

"Antidepressant." He paused and looked down at the cherry-colored laminate floor and then back at me. "See ... I used to get bullied when I was a kid for having the best things in life: the new Jordans, the new designer coats, latest game systems and what have you. Niggas would..."

"Jay"

"What yo?"

"I would prefer it if you wouldn't use that word."

"What word?"

"Nigga."

"Why?"

"Because it's a derogatory term."

"Black people use it all the time. And besides, I didn't mean it in that context that you're thinking of, so chill, bruh."

"That's beside the point ... it's an ignorant word, and I would highly appreciate it if you don't use it."

"Man ... anyways," he said, returning back to his story, "dudes would jump me when I was a kid walking home from school just to take my shit. I was a scrawny kid back then." I looked at Vijay's lean, six-foot, muscular frame, trying to imagine him as a short, skinny kid.

"Do you want to see a picture?" he asked as if he was reading my mind.

"Sure."

He came back with an old Kodak picture of him wearing a Boy Scout uniform, brown khaki shorts and a short-sleeved shirt with a red handkerchief wrapped around his neck.

"Awww ... look at you here. I can't believe this is you," I said. He smiled, staring down at the picture. "And look at your hair!" I exclaimed.

"I know ... I know ... it was a bit long."

"You actually look Indian here." His hair was straight and cut above the ears. It looked like a mop cut.

"Who are those people in the background?" He pinched the photo and scrutinized it as if it was his first time seeing it.

"Oh, I'm surprised you could see them, it's a bit blurry. That's my mother and stepfather."

"You guys looked happy here."

"Yeah, those were the good 'ol days," he said, staring dreamily at the picture. I could only assume that things had changed when his sister was born. I consulted my watch and saw it was 2:00 a.m. I didn't want the night to end, but I had to get up early for work. I told Jay that I should be going. He looked as if he wanted me to stay, but I wasn't sure. He walked me to the door and said I must give him the recipe to the clam soup. He also said it was the best dish I made to date, which made me smile.

8

Vijay

There was a knock at the door, and when I opened it Pierre was standing there with a bag of groceries. I grabbed a few bags from him and placed them on the kitchen counter. Earlier I had offered to go to the store to pick up the ingredients for tonight's dinner, but he insisted he'd go since tonight was a special meal. I didn't know what homeboy had up his sleeve until he unearthed groceries from the plastic bags.

"We're allowed to splurge tonight, right, Vijay?" he asked, holding up a block of butter, wrapped in gold foil.

"Yeah. Of course."

"I'm making soul food tonight," he said, placing a big can of peaches and two boxes of already-made Pillsbury pie dough on the kitchen counter. "I'm not going to spin all day in the kitchen fighting with pie crust. So these babies here are going to save me a lot time."

"Do you need any help?" I asked.

Pierre placed a finger on his full lips and said, "Boil some water for the macaroni."

Once the noodles were cooked, Pierre drained and placed them in a big silver bowl, which he grabbed from his apartment. I stood there watching him add a half stick of butter to the steamy noodles, two cups of sharp cheddar cheese, and a half cup of evaporated milk. For seasoning, he added a teaspoon of salt and coarse black pepper. He then poured the creamy mixture into a baking dish and added more cheese on top. He grabbed a red spice from the cabinet, which had me skeptical. He looked at me and told me it was smoked paprika. It was more for aesthetic purposes than taste, he assured me. He sprinkled the red spice on top, and then covered the baking dish with aluminum foil. He placed it in a 350-degree oven and set the stove timer for forty-five minutes.

I stood there watching him dance from the stove, to the counter, to the spice cabinet. He placed a few pieces of chicken thighs and legs into a big Ziploc bag that contained white flour and spices like garlic powder, salt, black pepper, and paprika. Once the oil became hot, he gently placed a drumstick into the pan. The oil sizzled, crackled, and popped. Pierre stood back until the first piece settled in the hot oil. He then added the rest. After he flipped the chicken in the pan, he strolled to the kitchen counter to a bowl of cooked potatoes cut into small cubes, which I had helped peel.

"What is this you making yo?"

"My sister's famous potato salad. Nobody makes a mean potato salad like my sister, Deloris," he said, cracking and peeling a few boiled eggs.

"I've never had this dish before."

"Well, today is your lucky day."

As he spoke, I felt my stomach rumble with hunger. After the food was done, he had everything laid out on the counter: Fried chicken, candied yams topped with pecans, macaroni and cheese, potato salad, and peach cobbler for desert. Everything looked and smelled so fucking amazing. I fixed myself a plate and instantly fell in love with the potato salad, which was smooth and creamy.

"What makes this taste so good?" I asked.

"You will probably laugh if I tell you this, but the secret ingredient is Miracle Whip."

"Ha! Really yo?"

"Yeah. That's the trick. Most people use mayonnaise, but Deloris hates it. She thinks it tastes like glue. So she uses Miracle Whip and a dash of yellow mustard for a spicy kick."

Next I tried the baked mac and cheese, which had a nice bubbly cheesy crust at the top. As I scooped some onto my plate, I noticed it had an eggy custard consistency. It was good. Once I polished that off, we cut into the peach cobbler, the dish I was most anticipating. The aromas of warm cinnamon and nutmeg ignited my hunger once again. Pierre placed a scoop of French vanilla ice cream on my piece before I took a bite. The crust was flaky, and the peach filling was buttery and sweet. Pierre smiled and said, "Vanilla extract and butter is the key."

After we finished stuffing our faces, we sauntered over to the sofa and plopped ourselves on it like two sumo wrestlers. I locked my hands behind my head and watched Pierre reach for a *Men's Health* magazine. He flipped through it and asked why some pages were dog-eared. I told him I was hoping we could try some more recipes from it. He nodded, tossed the magazine back onto the coffee table, and picked up another issue with a shirtless white guy wearing dark denim jeans on the cover. I wondered if white guys were Pierre's type. I still hadn't seen the guy he was supposedly seeing. I suddenly started to feel jealous of how long he was staring at the cover. I don't know why I was trippin'.

"You find him attractive?"

"Who?"

"The guy on the cover." I pointed to the magazine he was holding. He looked at me, confused, probably wondering why I was asking him such a ridiculous question.

"He's okay. I was trying to figure out where I saw him from."

"That's Ryan Gosling ... from the movie *The Notebook*. He's good-looking, no?" The last remark made Pierre turn and stare at me.

"Wait a minute. You judge guys on their looks?"

"Yeah yo, what's wrong with that?"

"I didn't know straight boys judge each on their looks."

"Well ... I wouldn't do it in a locker room, if that's what you're implying. But there isn't nothing wrong complimenting another guy."

"You don't find that a bit gay?"

"Naw bruh."

"Interesting."

"What's so interesting?" I asked, staring at him.

"It's just that I've never heard you compliment another guy before. That's all."

"Oh."

We fell silent for a moment. I still wondered what kind of guys he liked. Did he like fat or athletic? Short or tall? Asian, white, or black guys? For some reason I needed to know what type of guy Pierre went for. What floated his boat. Since we'd known

CONFUSED SPICE

each other, we never spoke about his interest in men, which made Pierre even more interesting. I leaned forward, placing my elbows on my knees and taking the magazine out of his hands.

"We're going to play a little game. I'm going to flip through this magazine, and you going to tell me what kind of guy you find attractive."

"What? You're kidding, right?"

"No ... I'm serious."

"Why does it matter who I find attractive in this magazine?" He looked really uncomfortable with where I was taking this.

"I'm sorry, homie. I just wanted to know what kind of guys you get down with, that's all."

"Jay, I really don't have a type. Can we just leave it at that?" he said, rising off the sofa. I rose up too, standing in front of him.

"Do you need help wrapping up the food?" He asked

I turned and looked toward the kitchen. I definitely needed a hand wrapping up all that food. I asked if he wanted to take some with him. He declined and said he was watching his figure. Even though the food was mad delicious, I decided to take the leftovers to work tomorrow. My personal trainer had me on a low-carb, high-protein diet, and this feast didn't fit his plan.

After we saran-wrapped the food, I walked Pierre to his apartment and thanked him for cooking soul food for me. He said no problem, anytime. I stood in the hallway until he closed the door behind him. I lingered there for a minute before returning to my apartment.

After doing some reading and research on Buddhism at Ryerson University's library, I decided to take a stroll down Yonge Street

45

to a T-Shirt shop that says "You think it, we ink it!". They sold crazy T-shirts. I wanted to buy Pierre something special for cooking me that feast the other day. In the window I saw this hot pink shirt that said *Food Before Dudes*. I thought Pierre would get a kick out of it. I walked into the store and told the white guy with scraggly blonde hair what size I needed. He found the shirt in a small on the top shelf at the back of the store and asked if I needed anything else. I said no and followed homeboy to the register, shouldering my black duffle bag stuffed with spiritual and intellectual books. As I dug into my back pocket for my wallet, the sales guy asked, "You got a hot girl, eh?"

"What, bruh?"

"Based on the size of this shirt, I'll take it you got a hot girl or trying to get into those panties." He grinned.

"Yeah man, whatever. Can I have my receipt," I said, not entertaining this joker. He ripped the receipt from the printer and placed it in the plastic bag along with the shirt. As I was walking out, he still wore a stupid grin. I made my way down Yonge to Bloor, bumping into people along the way. I didn't understand why people couldn't step to the side when Vijay Khakwani was coming through.

I walked into Saks Fifth Avenue and saw Pierre folding clothes, wearing all black and a necktie. I called out his name, and he turned around with a surprised look. He started toward me in a brisk walk and I met him halfway.

"What are you doing here, Jay?" he said, looking nervously around.

"I wanted to see where you work, and besides, I got you something yo." I handed him the shopping bag. He took it and pulled out the pink shirt. He wore a skeptical expression with eyebrows

CONFUSED SPICE

bunched and lines gathering on his forehead. I couldn't tell if he liked it or hated it. I stood there confused as fuck until he spoke.

"A hot pink shirt?" he said, finally looking up at me, holding the shirt stretched out with both hands.

"Yeah man. I thought you would like it."

"How gay do you think I am?" he said with a chuckle, holding the shirt against his chest for size. It looked a bit too small for him, but he didn't say so.

"I saw the shirt and thought of you. Is it cool. Do you like it? I can go back and..."

"No, I'm just joking. It's fine. Thanks for the gift. How did you know where I worked?

"You told me over dinner one night. However, you didn't tell me the location, but I knew where. There's only one Saks in downtown Toronto. Besides, I was in the area and thought to pay you a visit before I head back to Scarborough."

"Oh ... but what compelled you to buy me this gift?"

"Just for teaching me how to cook and preparing that amazing feast yo."

"My pleasure, Jay. You didn't have to buy me anything though. I enjoy teaching you how to throw down in the kitchen," said Pierre with a big smile.

"That's good to hear, because I want to ask you if you want to cook tonight, that is if you don't have any plans," I said, leaning against an Armani Exchange clothes rack.

"Well ... I have cooking class after work, but I finish at nine tonight."

"Would ten work?"

"Yeah, that time works just fine."

"Great yo, see you at ten."

47

9

Pierre

It was eleven at night. The elevator slid open, and I stepped onto my floor. I heard Drake blaring from Vijay's apartment. *Yes! He's home and not asleep.* My insides were doing somersaults. There was a bus detour on my way back home from cooking class, and I was hoping and praying that Jay wouldn't be asleep. I thought it was sweet of him to drop by my job today to give me an appreciation gift. My heart skipped a beat when I saw his beautiful mahogany face as he strode into Saks. At first I thought I was hallucinating until his smooth voice filled my ears. I must admit it was pretty embarrassing for him to see me what I do all day. Folding clothes sucks. I wanted him to have only memories of us cooking and me looking sexy in my skinny jeans, not serving rude-ass needy customers. I still didn't know what he did for a living. I knocked on the door, and within seconds he

CONFUSED SPICE

answered it wearing a skin-tight black wife-beater with his chest
and arms glistening with a thin layer of sweat.

"Hey, Jay, did I catch you at the wrong time?"

"Nah, man, not at all. Come in. What you have there?"

"I got something for you." I handed him a white box.

"What is this?" He smiled.

"Just open it."

"*Yooo!* Chocolate croissants."

"I made them in class today."

"Thanks, man." He took one out the box and took a hefty
bite. "This is delicious," he said with his mouth stuffed. "I just
put on coffee. Would you like some?"

"Sure."

He sauntered into the kitchen, set the box of croissants
on the counter, and opened up the cabinet, unearthing two
ceramic cups. I strolled into the living room and saw a plastic
dummy in the middle of room where the coffee table used
to be and boxing gloves with the name *Everlast* printed across
them lying on the sofa. I picked them up. They were relatively
warm.

"Do you box?" he asked from the kitchen.

"Not at all. I'm not fond of sports."

"Really?" He handed me a cup of coffee.

"Yeah. Just isn't my thing. Sorry to be such a big disappointment." I took a sip from my cup. The coffee was very strong. This
would definitely have me wired all night. Perhaps that was his
intention. He strolled back to the kitchen and took another bite
of his chocolate croissant that was sitting on a saucer.

"Bruh, this is really good. You have to teach me how to make
this. You should pursue this cooking thing as a career. You
are such a great cook, and that's real talk yo." He finished the

croissant and washed it down with his coffee. He then strode toward me.

"I'll tell you what, Pierre, if you teach me how to make these delicious chocolate croissants, I'll teach you how to box. Deal?"

"I don't see how that's a deal, given that I don't like sports, but I'm game."

"That's what I like about you, always down for anything."

I smiled inwardly.

"Was that what you were doing before I interrupted?"

"Yeah, I had to let off some steam." A few creases formed across his forehead. A thin layer of sweat still glistened on his smooth chest. I gripped my cup harder, feeling my manhood rising. "Now put those gloves on. Let me see what you got?" I reluctantly put down my cup on the glass coffee table and shoved on the gloves. They were tight for my big hands.

"Alright, Pierre, I want you to hit me in my stomach as hard as you can."

"Are you crazy? I'm not hitting you, and besides, there's a boxing dummy here. Now move out of the way and let me at this thing."

"No, I want you to learn this way. The good way for you to learn is to hit something real, something with emotion, something that can feel your strength, your blow, your damage. So come on and let me see what you got." He stood rigidly with his stomach muscles tightened. His black warm-up shorts hung on his hips in that sort of sexy way, which made his stomach look longer and leaner. I swallowed hard and tightened my fists. He smiled and gave me a wink. I pulled back my arm and gave him a blow on his side. He laughed. "Come on man, harder." He slapped me lightly upside the head, which made me a little upset and flushed in the face. My second punch was harder and

CONFUSED SPICE

swifter, but it did not seem to faze him. He hit me again, and I punched him a little harder. This process went on for a while.

"Okay, Jay, I had enough. I thought you were teaching me how to box, not using me as punching bag as well."

"Take off the gloves and hand them over."

"Huh?" I was perplexed, but I did what he said. He slipped them on effortlessly, as if they were second skin.

"Now, cover your face with your arms." I was apprehensive but was still game. He punched the side of my head, hitting my ear. "Come on man ... block." I tried to dip and dive like I saw him do just a few minutes ago, but I failed miserably. The blows kept coming fast and furious.

"Okay, Jay, enough. This is not my cup of tea. I just wanted to drop off those croissants. I didn't come over here to get my ass handed. I will let you continue with your boxing. I'm out." I picked up my coat, heading toward the door. He blocked me from leaving.

"I actually was going to meditate now. Would you like to join me?" I saw the pleading in his dark-lashed eyes for me to stay. This guy was confusing me. Why did he crave my company? I couldn't be the only friend in his life. I mean, he was absolutely gorgeous and interesting.

"Sure, Jay, I'll stay a little longer. I didn't know you meditated."

"I am full of surprises."

"So you are." I laughed. "But I've never meditated before."

"There's always the first time for everything." He smiled. "Let's do it in my bedroom."

What! Oh sweet Jeezus! Is he serious? Why can't we do it in the living room? Is this really happening? But I decided not to ask questions and go with the flow. I followed him into his bedroom and saw posters of Buddha and LeBron James taped above his bed.

51

"You're a Buddhist?"

"Not exactly. My family actually follows Islam, with the exception of my stepfather, who is agnostic. I decided to take a different spiritual path. I just recently got into this religion. I find it works best for me. But I wouldn't consider myself a Buddhist, at least not yet." He placed a couple of blue yoga mats on the carpeted floor and sat on one with his legs folded. I followed suit. He wanted to sit face to face so I could watch him demonstrate the breathing techniques of meditation. We were a few inches apart, with our knees slightly touching. I inhaled deeply and smelled the sweet musk of his body. It was euphoric.

"Now man, close your eyes and say OM for ten minutes. Don't stop until I do." I shook my head in agreement, and the room all of a sudden fell into absolute silence. He started to chant the word. I followed and immediately felt ridiculous. I didn't even know what OM meant. I could've been saying "I'm a dumbass" in a different language for all I knew. I broke the meditation with a chuckle. "Man, what's the hell wrong with you, *son!*" he said in a fake New York accent.

"My bad, but we sound like a couple of impregnated cows giving birth."

Instead of taking offense, he smiled.

"Let me explain something to you, Pierre. Meditation is supposed to help us come in touch with our inner self and with the Universe.

"The Universe?"

"Yes, the Universe is alive and kicking and knows our deepest wishes and dreams and can bring forth those things if we choose to listen. That's where meditation comes in. To help us recognize our truest potential and to bring us to the present moment."

CONFUSED SPICE

"Okay. But why do we have to say Om to connect to this so-called Universe of ours?"

"Om calls forth silence."

"Why do you do this?"

"It helps me relax. I have a lot going on up here," he said, tapping the side of his head. "So let's try it again. You must concentrate to find your sweet spot," he said with a grin.

"My sweet spot?" I cocked my head.

"Yeah, that empty space between you and your thoughts. To get there you will have to forge through the confused space."

"And what's in this empty space?"

"That's for you to discover," he said, boring his dark eyes into my own. We slowly closed our eyes and resumed chanting. I slightly peeked through my lashes and saw his athletic chest rise and fall like a warrior preparing for battle. I assumed he'd found his sweet spot, but I was having difficulty finding mine. His posture was straight and his breaths were slow and steady. I could feel his warm breath lightly brushing against my face. I looked at his exposed arms and muscular chest, wanting to reach out to touch and taste them. The room's light added a sexy sheen to his mahogany complexion, making it a rich cinnamon dolce latte color that I wanted to drink to the very last drop. I felt the blood in my manhood stiffen with sensual delight. The silence in the room made our bodies connect more on a stimulating intellectual and spiritual level. I wanted to know more about this mysterious guy: his troubles, his dreams, his deepest desires, his pain. It seemed as if he was running away from something, something that I couldn't put my finger on. Why was he so secretive? Why was he so shut off from the rest of the world? What was he not telling me? I already knew about his drug hustle. That part of his life was over for sure. I knew he was bullied in school for having the best in life. Perhaps that was the reason why he boxed — to defend himself. Perhaps meditation helped him to deal with his troubling past. He opened his eyes, and I pretended to open mine.

"How do you feel?"

"I feel light," I lied.

"See?" He smiled.

I consulted my watch, which read a quarter past twelve. "Woah, it's getting really late. I know you might have work tomorrow."

"Yeah, but it's not till one in the afternoon."

I still didn't know what he did for a living. "Where do you work?"

"Well ... I recently lost my job as a bar-back at a nightclub downtown."

"A what? You did bareback? Isn't that sexual?"

"Nah bruh, I said bar-back ... it's a bartender's assistant." My lips formed an O, and he continued, "I bussed tables and stocked liquor."

"What happened?"

"I got into it with the bartender, that's what happened. He was a complete ass. Always ordering me around like I was some kind of punk. I punched that dude in his bearded fat face and told him I quit this piece of shit. He had the bouncers toss me out onto Queen Street, embarrassing me in front of some fine honeys waiting to get into the club. I should've punched that nig — I mean ... that dude twice. But anyway, that's under the bridge now, and I got a new gig working at Foot Locker," he said plainly. "It's not the most exciting job, but at least I get the latest kicks half price." He smiled. "Come on. Let's get something to drink. I'm thirsty yo."

CONFUSED SPICE

We rose and headed to the kitchen. He poured some lemonade into two plastic dollar-store cups, and we strode over to the ancient sofa. "You know what, Pierre? I really enjoy hanging around you. I am not going to lie. I used to be a homophobe, but when I met you, you changed all that."

"That's good, Jay." Now I knew we would be nothing but friends.

"So, how is your boyfriend? When am I going to meet him?"

"I don't have a boyfriend."

"But I thought..."

"I know, but it didn't work out."

"Do you want to talk about it?"

"Not really."

"Well ... don't worry, you will find someone soon. I'm sure of it."

"What makes you so sure?" I asked incredulously.

"Because you are very attractive, Pierre," he said, giving me a hypnotic gaze with those long-lashed eyes sending a rumbling pleasure within me. Then he took a quick sip of his drink. *He finds me attractive?* It was this kind of shit that put me back in a confused space. *Is he gay? Is he secretly living on the down low?* Or perhaps I was over-analyzing this. There's nothing wrong with a guy paying another guy a generous compliment, right? Why was Jay toying with my emotions? I saw something red flicker in my peripheral vision on the glass coffee table. Jay reached for his phone and read his missed calls and texts. I watched his face light up over a text. I wondered if his face lit up over my texts.

"What is it, Jay?"

"It's nothing."

"Don't lie. I know something is up," I said with an edge in my tone, almost sounding like a jealous girlfriend.

55

MATHIS BAILEY

"Well ... it's this girl named Tameka. I had a crush on her since I was, like, in the first grade yo."

I felt jealousy creep in.

"Have you told her how you felt?"

"Not really. I think I fell into the friend zone with her."

"I think you should tell her how you feel. You never know, she probably feels the same way about you."

"You think so?" he said, smiling widely.

"Yeah."

"This girl makes me really happy. It's just something about her."

"Do you know if she is seeing someone?"

"She's single. But she told me she isn't looking to get into anything serious because she wants to focus on her studies. That is another reason I like her. She isn't a Scarborough hood rat. She is really smart and motivated. This girl has it all. Everything a guy could ask for. I think I'm going to take your advice and ask her out."

My stomach went south. "Yeah, man, keep me posted. Well, Jay, I have to get going," I said, feeling like a wounded whale that got harpooned in the chest, finally realizing I had competition. I rose, and he followed suit. I made my way toward the door while he jogged to open it. We stood in front of each other like two strangers meeting for the first time, not knowing what to say.

"Thanks for tonight, even though we didn't cook anything yo." He half-smiled. "It's always great talking to you," he said as he stared at me, probably sensing my melancholy mood.

"Same here, Jay. Have a good night." I turned and started toward my apartment, thinking about the finality of our potential romance. He was giving his attention and energy to someone else. We would be nothing more than friends. He didn't want me

56

the way I wanted him. Why waste any more time pretending we were something more.

"Yo, Pierre!" he shouted over my shoulder. I turned around, standing between our apartments. "My parents are having their annual soiree this weekend at their place. It's going to be mad food there. Food I think you will enjoy. Do you want to come?" He flashed a million-dollar smile that I couldn't resist. What was it about this guy that had a hold over me? A hypnotic spell that I couldn't shake off.

"Sure, Jay. I will be there."

Fall was coming to an end, but the sun was high in the sky, and the temperature was mild with a light breeze.

The taxi made a left on Markham Road and took it all the way down to the suburbs. The homes got bigger as we drove. The taxi pulled over at the end of a cul de sac in front of a two-story peach-colored house. I dug into my pocket, unearthed two twenties, and paid the Ethiopian driver. As I made my way to the door, trepidation bounced around in my stomach like a metallic ball in a pinball machine. A fluffy white cat with piercing blue eyes appeared on the stoop and stood guard at the door. I rang the doorbell, which made a sing-song sound. A few seconds later, a beautiful woman opened it, wearing a cream silk blouse tucked into dark blue jeans that accentuated her feminine curves. She was incredibly in shape. Her skin was as smooth as Canadian maple butter. Her black hair was cut around the ears, and it made her neck appear long and elegant. She brought a slender hand up to her pearl necklace and looked at me from the feet up, as if sizing me for an Italian suit.

MATHIS BAILEY

"You must be Vijay's friend, ...Pierre is it?" she asked in a cultured tone. "He told me so much about you. Do come in." I couldn't believe Jay had been talking about me to his parents. That was more than my fiancé, Dre, had ever done. His parents didn't even know I existed. I stood in the foyer looking up at the high ceiling. A grandiose glass chandelier hung in the middle, giving the illusion of dripping crystals. The house was furnished with white furniture on marble floors that shined as if it had been scrubbed and polished all day by a tireless hand. A Tom Ford gift box sat on a white chair near the entrance of the door. A gift, perhaps, from one of her guests.

"This is for you." I handed her a bottle of red wine, and she brought a hand to her pearls and looked at me as if I was giving her a murder weapon. "Sorry dear, my family doesn't drink wine. We're Muslims. Vijay should have told you."

"Oh! I'm sorry, he did. I just forgot. My apologies, Mrs...."

"Mrs. Morrison, call me Mrs. Morrison." She wore a smug look at my blunder. I guessed she'd changed her last name when she remarried to Vijay's stepfather. I clutched the wine back against my chest, not quite sure what to do with it. She led me out onto the patio, where the rest of the guests were congregated.

As we stepped onto the spacious patio, I overheard people chatting about taking a trip up north to their cottages while the good weather lasted. I scanned the crowd for Jay but couldn't find him. On the lawn there was a white man at the grill flipping burgers and poking sausages. He wore khaki shorts and a loud floral shirt — the only person that looked reasonably comfortable. Was he Vijay's stepfather? A few minutes later I was shown to the patio table and introduced by Mrs. Morrison two beautiful young ladies.

58

CONFUSED SPICE

"Pierre, meet Navaan, our next-door neighbor, and ... I'm sorry, what's your name, darling?"

"Suhana," said the young woman in a soft voice.

"What a lovely name, dear. Can I get anyone anything to drink?" We all put up a hand. "Okay, I'll be back. I will let you all get better acquainted."

Once Mrs. Morrison disappeared, I decided to break the ice.

"So Navaan, how long have you known the Morrisons?"

"All my life," said Navaan, tossing back her long micro braids with a flick of her hand. She was wearing a flowing bohemian dress that looked as if it was from Forever 21. She was a sistah with a beautiful clear toffee-nut complexion. "My girl here just tagged along." I looked over at Suhana, who seemed bored. She wore a fitted, knee-length cream-colored dress with sleeves that stopped below the elbow. Her jet-black hair was straight and perfectly parted, which contrasted well with her honey complexion. My guess was that she was Indian. "What about you?" asked Navaan.

"I'm a friend of Vijay's. We live in the same apartment building. This my first time meeting his family."

"Speaking of Vijay, where is that crazy boy?" said Navaan. I shrugged. It was odd that Jay wasn't here. His mother came back to the table with glasses of non-alcoholic sangria. I took a sip and enjoyed the refreshing taste of fresh strawberries and blood oranges mixed with San Pellegrino. Navaan asked for the recipe, and Mrs. Morrison was more than happy to tell her. It was so delicious that I didn't miss the alcohol. I looked up at Mrs. Morrison and noticed she wore an exasperated look. She mumbled a few inaudible words under her breath.

"Vijay seems to be running late," she said. "But he will be here shortly." She tried to muster up a smile before leaving to attend to her other guests, who I assumed were her colleagues.

59

"She looks really upset," I said.

"Oh, Vijay always does things like this," said Navaan.

"Things like what?"

"Things that tick his mother off."

"How come?"

She pursed her glossed lips as if she had already said too much. "I don't know. They've had this love and hate relationship ever since I've known them." A few minutes later, Jay appeared, looking handsome in a form-fitting black sport blazer wearing underneath a crisp white V-neck T-shirt with Zara jeans that made him look like he just jumped off the cover of *GQ* magazine. His hair was freshly cut, adorned with a fitted Blue Jays cap that rested askew on his hairline. He flashed a million-dollar smile that made the guests forget about his tardiness.

"You guys came!" he joyously exclaimed. "Pierre, you never seem to let me down. I am happy that you were able to come." Mrs. Morrison came stomping toward the patio with a tirade bubbling at her wine-colored lips.

"Vijay, may I see you in the house?"

"Whatever you have to say can wait until my guests leave," he said, not taking his eyes off us. She cut him with a glare and was about to give him a good talking-to but looked our way and thought better of it. She huffed and strutted into the house. She came back out carrying a tray of thin slices of prosciutto and cubed smoked Gouda cheese stabbed with toothpicks. A little girl wearing a flower-printed dress followed behind her, balancing a silver tray like a duchess in training.

"Who is the little girl?" I asked.

"That's my little sis, Vanessa." I looked back and forth between the little girl and Jay. They looked nothing alike. I also noticed Jay had the darkest complexion in his family.

CONFUSED SPICE

"She is getting so big and more beautiful every time I see her. How old is she now?" asked Navaan.

"She's twelve. Come on, Pierre. Let me introduce you properly to my family." As we strolled onto the lawn, kids weaved between us, chasing one another. I placed my hands deeply into my pockets as we made our way over to the grill. I suddenly became nervous again. I could only imagine some of the things that his parents were going to ask: *What do you do for a living? Where are you from? Why did you move to Canada? Are you married?* I wondered if Jay had told them everything about me. Jay was always full of surprises. He probably was using me for heavy ammo against his mother.

From a distance I saw Mrs. Morrison place a hand on her husband's shoulder as we approached. I felt beads of sweat form on my forehead. *Holy crap, what am I going to say?* I could say the most idiotic things in the most awkward situations.

"So this is the neighbor that I've been telling you guys about. He's a great cook."

His dad turned, spatula in hand.

"So, you're the famous Pierre. Our son told us so much about you," he said, pushing up his wire-framed glasses with his hairy knuckles. "I heard you were a professional cook, eh? What do you make?"

"Oh, I wouldn't consider myself a professional, but I make almost everything. I mostly enjoy making Indian food, chicken tikka and butter chicken."

"You don't say? I love Indian food myself, but my wife here isn't too fond of it. Isn't that right, honey?" He gave her a nudge on her hip, which provoked her to smack her painted maroon lips. He continued, "I remember when we took a trip to Guyana, I must have dragged her to every hole-in-the-wall restaurant for spicy Indian food. She was furious with me for making her walk

61

MATHIS BAILEY

in such heat." He looked over to his wife. She frowned at the memory, poking at the juicy burgers that were oozing Gruyère cheese. "She wanted to kill me." He chuckled. Vijay stood there as if it was his first time hearing the story.

"I didn't know Indian food was so popular in Guyana," I said.

"Yes, dear, most of the population is made up of Indians," said Mrs. Morrison, finally contributing to the conversation. "Indians were brought over to Guyana as indentured workers. Most of them were tricked and kidnapped into slavery. But I don't want to bore you with a history lesson, darling. I took Caribbean studies while attending Ryerson University. Tell me, where did you go to school?"

Damn this nosy bitch. "Well, I went to Michigan University for Broadcast Journalism but didn't finish. When I moved here, I wanted to change professions. I feel my passion lies in the culinary arts, so I recently applied to George Brown." I sensed she wasn't impressed with my education, nor career path.

"I hear an accent in your voice. Where are you from?" asked Mrs. Morrison

"He's from Detroit. He's an American," Jay chimed in, sounding very proud, before I could speak.

"Oh! An American, eh?" his father said. "Where in the States have you visited?" I noticed every time I told someone I was from the States, they automatically assumed that I had traveled across the region, especially to New York City. I hated to dim their excitement.

"I'm sorry, but I didn't travel much when I lived in the States. I just visited neighboring places like Chicago and Ohio." *Does Ohio even count?* I thought. I only visited there to have a good time at Cedar Point, a wonderful amusement park I went to plenty of times on school trips. I never went sightseeing.

CONFUSED SPICE

"How is Detroit? I had always wanted to go to a Tigers game. It must be the biggest event in your city?" *Oh crap! This conversation isn't going well at all. I guess Jay didn't tell them about my aversion to sports.*

"Well ... the city is going through a recession, so it isn't a great place to be at the moment. A really good job is hard to find. But the Tigers are still a great team; I think you'd have fun at one of their games," I said, trying to sound upbeat. I looked at Mrs. Morrison, and I saw lines form across her forehead. I felt a question foaming at her maroon lips.

"What was your reason for coming to Canada?" she asked, boring her long-lashed eyes into mine like a hawk beginning to attack its prey. It was obvious that Jay hadn't told them about my sexual preference, unless they wanted to hear it out of my mouth. I looked at Jay for any censorship, but he looked as if he didn't care what incriminating words might spew from my lips.

"I came here to be close to a loved one," I decided to say.

"Oh, I assumed that all your family lived in Detroit," Mrs. Morrison said.

"Well ... they do. I meant my lover."

Jay's parents looked at me in silence. Mrs. Morrison continued with the inquisition.

"If you don't mind me asking, how did you obtain citizenship in this country?" I could sense the litigator in her was starting to emerge. I swallowed hard.

"My lover sponsored me. We are in the process of getting married." I saw the look on Vijay's face change. He only knew that I was seeing someone. He failed to delve further into my love life. He recovered the look on his face and stared back at his parents. Something told me we would be talking about this the moment we were out of his parents' presence.

63

There was a moment of silence until Mrs. Morrison spoke again. "Vijay, did you see that lovely young lady with Navaan? She is quite beautiful, isn't she? She reminds me a little of that black singer." She tapped her manicured finger on her lips and looked my way for help, but I shrugged in return. "Ah! Alicia Keys," she exclaimed. Jay looked back at the young ladies on the patio enjoying their non-alcoholic sangrias and stared at Suhana with new interest. I also thought she resembled Alicia Keys with her lustrous black hair cascading past her shoulders and framing her oval face. The only difference was Suhana was slimmer. "You should speak to that young girl while the evening is still young," his mother coaxed, sipping a glass of sparkling cider that she had sitting near the grill. Jay did not oppose the thought.

I looked around and saw an elderly Indian woman dressed in an apricot-colored chiffon sari mingling amongst the guests. Her hair was parted down the middle and pulled into an elegant bun at the nape of her neck.

"That's my grandmother," Vijay said. "Let me introduce you two." I was relieved to get away from the inquisition. "Nana, this is my friend and good neighbor, Pierre." The old woman looked at me warmly. The gold bangles on her wrinkled arm rattled like tiny bells as she shook my hand. She had a red dot in the middle of her forehead and spoke with an accent I couldn't place.

"How are you, dear? Are you having a nice time?"

"Yes, very much so, ma'am."

"Vijay, make sure your friend here gets something to eat."

"Yes, Nana." She fixed the *paloo* on her shoulder, patted Vijay on the back, and wobbled off to greet the arriving guests.

CONFUSED SPICE

"Your grandmother seems very nice," I said as we sauntered toward the garden away from the party. "I noticed she is the only person in your family who has an accent and looks traditional."

Jay laughed. "Yeah, she watches Hindi movies all the time and even speaks it."

"Do you know any Hindi?" He stopped walking and gave me an are-you-serious-look. "I'll take that look as a no." We laughed in unison. "Your mother seemed really upset with you earlier for being late."

"Whatever!" he said with a dismissive wave. "She is always upset about something."

"Oh," I managed to say. He looked at me as if I deserved an explanation since I was his guest.

"I was late because I got held up doing volunteer work downtown."

"Volunteer work? Doing what?" I asked, intrigued. Vijay's heart was always in the right place.

"I promised a friend that I would help her feed the homeless at a shelter at Yonge and College. So that's the reason why I was late yo. I should have planned my day better. I know everyone thought I was out getting my hair cut or something."

"Yeah, which looks good, by the way."

"Thanks. I got it freshly lined up this morning."

I laughed. "Jay, you really do have to work on your time management."

"I know. I know. I'm working on it," he said with a shameless grin across his beautiful cinnamon-mocha face. Then his expression suddenly became serious. "So, why didn't you tell me about your engagement?"

65

I fell silent for a moment. "You never asked. Besides, I didn't know you actually cared to hear about my personal life. It seems to freak you out."

"Nonsense, I'm a lot more open now."

"Um ... okay."

"So, when are you and homeboy getting, you know, married?"

"I don't know. It hadn't been decided yet."

"Do you love him?"

"Huh? Where did that question come from?"

"Sorry, I shouldn't have asked you that." We fell silent for a moment until he spoke again. "Pierre..."

"Yes," I said, looking warily at him, hoping he wouldn't ask any other personal questions about my love life. At this point we were off away from the crowd, standing near a thick patch of pines and bushes. The sun was setting, painting the sky a blush of purple and pink. I wondered what Jay was feeling deep within himself. What were his desires? I wanted to taste his perfect outlined lips at this very moment. He took a deep breath and stared into the sunset; the light made his dark brown eyes a bright amber. "What are you thinking, Jay?"

"Well..." He turned to me. "Ever since I met you, you've been a pleasure to be with, turning my darkest days into bright ones. You're always happy yo. I like that about you." He smiled, staring intensely into my eyes. "And I sense you see me as who I really am. See me in a way that no one else understands or want to see me. It's been a long time since I exposed myself to anyone, Pierre. I feel as if you are my best friend." I had no idea where Jay was going with this. What kind of best friend was I that didn't tell one of my closest friends I was getting married? Best friends? Fuck this bullshit. I needed to know the truth.

CONFUSED SPICE

"Jay, I am glad I've made your life a bit better. I've always tried to be there for you. But I feel you are keeping something from me?" Vijay's face twisted and then all of sudden darkened.

"I told you everything that there is to know about me."

But do you have strong, passionate feelings for me? I know you do, I wanted to say but couldn't force the words from my lips. My heart yearned to hear him say it.

"Pierre ... I..."

"Yes, Jay?" I urged him on, leaning forward in full anticipation. He croaked and looked into the direction of the party. I followed his gaze and saw his mother eyeing us, feigning not paying us much attention. She seemed to have a hold on Jay, and I wished I knew what it was. "Jay, finish what you were saying." He looked back at me like I was a different person. Not the same person he was talking to a few seconds ago.

"Pierre, I just think you are an awesome friend," he said. "Now, if you will excuse me, I have to attend to the rest my guests. Help yourself to the food." He trucked off as I stood there thinking about the words that he'd wanted to say but couldn't. I stared at his mother, who wore a triumphant smile, as if she'd heard everything said between us. I pulled my phone from my pants pocket and keyed in a number for a cab. I needed to get out of there and have a real drink.

67

10

Vijay

It was a quarter past ten at night. I had survived another one of my mother's wretched parties of random people asking me invasive questions: *When are you going to get married? What do you do for a living? How much do you make doing what you do?* After the last guest left, I went into the kitchen to help my grandmother put away the food. Moments later, my mother and Frank entered the kitchen. Frank poured himself a cup of organic coffee while my mother took over cleaning up. She told Nana to rest and that she would bring her a hot cup of Darjeeling tea. Nana wiped her hands on the dishtowel that hung on the stove's handle. She patted me on the back and wished me a good night. I looked at my mother, who wore a heavy frown. I wondered what was eating her. She couldn't be still upset with me for showing up late. I wondered what she thought of Pierre. He was totally different from the lowlifes I used to run the streets with. I wanted to show my mother that I had changed.

"I never want to see that boy step another foot in this house again," she said sternly.

"Huh?"

"You know what your mother means, Vijay," said Frank, pushing up his glasses.

"Pierre? Are you guys serious?"

"He's a homosexual, Vijay," said my mother

"You out of all people should have sympathy for him, given that you dedicate your life to defending people without a voice."

"Vijay, this isn't an issue to be trifled with."

"She's right, son," said Frank, standing next to her with a hand on her shoulder, holding the coffee in the other.

"No, what this is, is a bunch of bullshit."

"Watch your mouth young man. Have respect for your mother," said Frank, taking a step forward. Burning blood started to course through my veins like snake venom. I felt my face getting hot. I couldn't believe what I was hearing.

"So he isn't allowed in this house because he's gay? Unfuckin' believable."

"I'm not losing my son to a flaming queer."

My eyebrows shot up. "What do you mean losing me to him?"

"Don't play naive, Vijay," she said. "You don't see the way he stares at you?" I kind of sensed that Pierre might have a thing for me, but part of it was my fault for teasing and leading him on with things I said and did. I remembered when we went out for Popeye's chicken one evening and brought it back to my place, and I leaned toward him and asked if I could have his thighs, with a little lilt in my voice. The look on his face was priceless. He didn't know what to say; he just stared at me with his almond-shaped eyes like a cute deer in the headlights. Right then I wanted to sex his lips. I looked at my parents and then looked away as if they saw through the veil of my indecent thoughts. My mother sighed and sauntered toward me. She placed her pale hand on my face, causing me to look down at her. "I would like for you to have an arranged marriage."

I lowered her hand in disbelief. "You can't be serious."

"I'm very serious."

I looked at Frank in disbelief as he nodded.

"No ... no ... NO!"

"It's for the best," said my mother. "It's time for you to grow up and take on some responsibility. And I think you settling down will solve it."

"But I even don't have a proper job. How am I going to support a family? Let alone buy a house?"

"Frank and I already discussed that. We will pay the first two years of your rent until you finish college. Or you and your wife can live with us until you two stand on your own. It's very common in our Indian culture."

"*Indian* culture? This is insane! When did Guyanese start having arranged marriages?"

"Just because your grandparents migrated to Guyana from India, it doesn't mean they gave up their heritage."

"But you two even didn't have an arranged marriage. My stepfather is white for crying out loud." I pointed at Frank to state the obvious. Frank and my mother looked at each other and clearly saw I had a point, but they were prepared for it.

"Vijay, my situation was different. I had to make sacrifices."

"Oh really, like what sacrifices?" I asked, crossing my arms against my chest.

"I'm not going to get into it. I've made a decision, and that is final."

"No, I will not have an arranged marriage, plain and simple. Besides, when did you all of sudden care about tradition and customs?"

"Vijay, I should have been more strict with you when you were growing up instead of spoiling you rotten with all those American clothes and games. I should've taught you tradition and family values, like my parents tried to instill in me. But unfortunately, your grandfather died and I had to make the best decisions I could."

"And what does Nana have to say about this?"

"Actually, it was her idea," said my mother. She knew she had won a point. Everyone knew how much I loved and obeyed my grandmother. She was my everything. But I couldn't believe she was going along with this arranged marriage. I had to get to the bottom of this, fast. But I knew my grandmother was exhausted from chatting with all the guests today and probably wanted to rest. So I decided to speak with her some other time. Not wanting to hear more of what my mother had to say about the matter, I left the kitchen. I opened the door to the living room coat closet, unhooked my jacket from the wooden hanger, and headed out into the dark night.

11

Vijay

The next evening, I arrived at work late. My manager had a fucked-up expression on his chubby face. I strolled past him and toward the back to clock in, where mountains of shoeboxes were stacked to the ceiling. I took off my coat and threw it on a chair instead of hanging it in the employees' room. I walk back out front and noticed how packed the mall was. I guess people were doing their early Christmas shopping. For the past week this place had been like a zoo. I dreaded coming here and dealing with indecisive customers who couldn't make up their damn minds about what size shoe they could fit on their fat foot. I hated this place with a burning passion. I slapped hands with my boy Travis, a cool black guy with a thick Jamaican accent. He made me feel like a brotha. He was the one that got me brushing my hair mad crazy to get the sickest waves.

CONFUSED SPICE

His waves were tight. He was one of those dudes that brushed his hair with a wooden brush twenty-four seven. I tried to do the same to my short, spiky hair, but the waves refused to come. I even tried wearing a wave cap over night, but nothing. I hated my fucking hair. Travis and I had pictures of us all over Facebook looking like true homies. He gave me heads-up that today could be my last day working at Foot Locker. He was tipped off by the manager that my lateness was becoming an issue. To be honest, I didn't give a fuck about this job.

A young, slim black woman with red hair and pink nails approached me, chewing gum and pushing a stroller.

"May I help you, miss?" I asked.

"Can I get this in a size six?" she said rather demandingly.

"Sure." I took the pink-and-white Nike shoe, went to the back, and searched in the sea of orange boxes, perusing the white labels bearing the sizes. I found a box, but it was a six and a half. Oh well. I brought the shoe to the woman, who now was looking at another pair of shoes. "Here you are, ma'am, we only have a size six and a half."

"Oh no, that is too big," she said, screwing up her lips, uninterested in trying on the shoe. "Instead, can I try on these Pumas in the same size?" She was holding a shoe by the tips of her long, painted pink nails, as though it was contagious.

"Sure thing," I said with a slight edge in my voice. I strolled toward the back with a gangsta step in my walk. *This bitch can't boss me around. Hell no. I won't let her.* I found the shoes she requested, but they were mounted all the way at the top. I grabbed the ladder and climbed up to retrieve the size, trying to steady myself on this flimsy piece of shit. I climbed back down with the box tucked underneath my arms as the ladder wobbled and shook. When I got back to the front of the store, the chick had disappeared. She

MATHIS BAILEY

was nowhere to be seen. "Yo, Travis, did you see that crazy chick I was helping?"

"Nah, guy, perhaps she went to *dez*-restroom," he said in his slight Jamaican accent.

"You got to be kidding me," I exclaimed. I felt a tap on my shoulder, and I turned around with an exasperated look. *WHAT THE FUCK DO YOU WANT NOW.* It was a young black kid holding up a pair of new-release black Jordans; I owned a pair myself. This kid had taste.

"Can I please get these in a size seven?" he said politely.

"Sure thing, little man. Just give me a sec while I put this box back."

As I made my way back to the front of the store, I saw the black woman, now complaining to my manager. I handed the little man the box and listened in on the conversation between this crazy chick and my manager. I took out the shoe, removed the crumpled brown paper tucked inside, and loosened up the laces, and handed to the little guy.

"Yes, ma'am. I understand … yes, I completely understand. Uh-huh."

"This is unacceptable. I've been waiting here, and he is serving someone else."

"I understand."

"Is this how you treat your customers?"

"No it isn't."

Out of frustration, I interrupted. I could tell it was about me and my work ethic. This chick better go somewhere else with her crazy shit.

"Are you still interested in trying on those shoes, ma'am?" I managed to say as politely as possible.

"This is the guy," she said, pointing to me.

"I beg yo pardon," I said.

CONFUSED SPICE

"You left me waiting all this time while you go help someone else."

"Are you serious?" I said, trying my best not to snap on this broad. "You were gone; I had no clue where you were."

"That's a lie," she said.

"So, you're telling me you didn't leave the store, ma'am?" I asked while my manager assessed the situation. He looked at me, then at her, remaining silent as we spoke.

"No, I was over there by the clothes, looking at a cute little workout shirt, while you took all day bringing back those pair of shoes that I asked for. You are a poor worker. I came in here once before, and the same thing happened. This is ridiculous. I need to talk to upper management."

"Ma'am, I am the manager," said Joe.

"Well, I suggest you deal with this matter."

"Man, you're trippin'," I said.

"Pardon me?" she said, smacking her lips.

"You heard me," I said with my arms folded against my chest.

"Vijay, can I see you in my office?" Joe said, trying to defuse the tension. Once we were in his office, he closed the door and took a seat behind his desk, which was strewn with employee name tags, pens, and opened packages of snacks. He took out a beige folder from the file cabinet and placed it before him. I stood standing with my arms folded. I hoped he wasn't taking this psychotic bitch's side, because if he did, I was going to flip a lid. I hated this fuckin' job. He unscrewed a half empty bottle of sweetened Lipton ice tea and took a big gulp. I waited for him to talk before I said anything. He waited to compose his thoughts then spoke deliberately.

"Vijay, lately I've been getting constant complaints about your actions here at Foot Locker. Do you care to explain yourself?"

75

"Explain myself?" *Does this fool know who I am? I'm Vijay Khakwani. Who does this punk think he's messin' with? He's roughly the same age as me. Me explaining my actions to a dickhead who wears his shirt tucked in his pants like a joker. Ha! That's classic.* I tried to think about the teaching from this spiritual book that I was reading to ease my anger, but no mantras or wise quotes came to mind. Nothing could make me think positive thoughts at this point. I was pissed the fuck off.

"Not only have I been getting countless complaints, but I have also been looking at your attendance, and it is atrocious. Fifteen call-offs and four no-shows within the past three months. I've been trying to work with you, but you're leaving me with no choice to let you go, Vijay."

"So you're firing me?" I said with my brows bent.

He sighed deeply. "Yes, I'm afraid so. I will have to ask you to sign a couple of forms for your termination." He handed me two pink slips. I took the papers, tore them in four pieces, tossed them into the stagnant air like confetti, and strode out.

I left the office without saying goodbye to that prick. I untucked my shirt and let it hang out over my black slanks in a careless fashion. I strode to the front of the store and gave the black woman a fucked-up look. Perhaps I shouldn't be so mad at her; she was actually doing me a huge favor. I gave my boy Travis a dap on the fist and told him, "Peace." And threw up deuces with two fingers. I walked out with a fuck-this-shit strut.

A few minutes later I was cruising down the 401, bumping "99 Problems" by Jay Z. Nothing seemed to be going my way. First this arranged marriage biz and now losing my job. Just fucking great. I turned up the radio more. I got a text from my mother asking me to pick up my little sis from school. I didn't know why she was always too fucking busy to do it herself. I turned up the music more and nodded my head to the beat. This shit was bang'n. I pressed on the accelerator, kicking up to one-forty kilometers per hour. *Fuck this life.* In my rear-view mirror I saw a cop car creeping up behind me. *Shit!* The light flashed, and I pulled over. I was handed a fat ticket for speeding and not wearing my seat belt. *Fuck!* I tossed the yellow ticket into the glove compartment, along with the rest of them.

Once in my apartment, I flicked on the kitchen light, having it be the only light source to brighten up the place. I pulled off my black-and-white Foot Locker shirt, flung it in the air, and kicked it once it fell to the floor. I opened up the refrigerator, drank from the orange juice carton, and carried it with me to the dimly lit living room window. I saw trees swaying in the late evening breeze while cars wheezed on by. Everything moved with purpose, except my life. I took a last swig from the carton and drew the blinds. I tossed the empty carton in the garbage and switched off the kitchen light. I plopped onto the couch and sat in complete darkness, pondering my next move. I guessed I would have to find another job first thing in the morning. I sat there, and a foggy sleep took hold, temporarily washing my worries away.

Through the thickness of silence, I heard keys jingling in the hallway. I leaped up like an alerted Bassett Hound with ears pointed. I stood in the darkness of my apartment, shirtless. I wondered if it was Pierre. I was suddenly craving his company. He always managed to make me feel better with his wit. Just thinking about him brought a smile to my face. My boy Pierre.

I looked around for my phone and saw it on the kitchen counter. I picked it up, and the screen lit up along with the time. It was 1:00 a.m. *Damn! it's late.* We'd stayed up this late before, but I'd never texted him to come by at this hour. I thought about sending him a text, but something told me I could wait to see him tomorrow. To get a quick Pierre fix, I scrolled through the old messages on my phone and read them. One read: *Indian food or Mexican tonight?* I replied: *Whatever you like, as long's I'm eating your cooking,* and he replied *You're so silly Jay.* I loved it when he said that. It tickled me in a way that I couldn't yet explain. I'd only felt this way once when I was in high school, when this dude used to tutor me. He was Indian and came from a traditional Hindu family. He was shy and quiet, but I knew he wanted me, the way he would look at me as I bit my lip trying to solve a math problem. I secretly found him attractive too. However, nothing happened between us. We just couldn't cross that line. I learned to suppress these wayward feelings. Now I was having them again. Pierre was getting to me. He was constantly on my mind, even when I was sexing up a hot babe.

I clicked on the Facebook app on my phone to see if there were any new messages in my inbox. I happened to stumble upon Pierre's page and read his status: *I had a wonderful day in cooking class. We learned how to make petite fours. They were so delicious. Now I'm feeling fat. Gym tomorrow, I guess.* I laughed and laid back on the sofa, and contemplated replying to his post. But what would I say? Instead I just liked it. He posted some pictures of him baking and cooking in class and all the desserts he made. He looked so happy. I noticed in one picture he appeared to be laughing with a Chinese-looking guy who seemed to be gay and interested in Pierre. He was feeding Pierre a buttery croissant dusted with powder sugar, and some got on Pierre's nose. I felt my left hand curling into a fist while I held my phone tighter. But I didn't think he was Pierre's type, so why was I trippin'? And why was I thinking about dudes anyway? Those neurotic thoughts needed to cease. I didn't know what neurotic meant until I heard my mother use it when I was a kid. She thought rap music was neurotic. I remember flipping the TV to BET, and she would tell me to turn that neurotic music off and hit the books.

I placed my phone on the coffee table, strode into my bedroom, and sprawled on the mattress, staring up at the white popcorn celling while thoughts swarmed in my head like fluttering moths. My life seemed to be going nowhere. *Why is it this hard? When will I find the river of enlightenment? When will I find my purpose in life? I can't go back to that dark place when I wanted to take my life with a bottle of pills.* My mind shifted to Pierre. I wondered what he was up to. I reached for my MacBook on the side table and powered it up. I logged back onto Facebook, and a new picture of Pierre appeared on my feed. He was rolling dough in his French pastry class. Should I like it? I hit the like button. I clicked on his page and saw another uploaded picture of him with a group of people wearing white hats and aprons, smiling. I instantly felt jealous. I wanted to be a part of his clique, his circle of friends. I wanted to be the center of his world. Be the one on his page for the world to see us together. I clicked off the laptop and thought to send Pierre a text, until I looked over at the clock on the nightstand, which read a quarter past one. I lay down and tossed over in bed. Tomorrow would come quick, and then I would see him.

12

Pierre

I yawned before sitting up in bed. I reached for my phone on the side table and noticed that Jay had sent me a text. He wanted me to come over at noon. I looked over at the clock on the side table. It was eleven. I replied *sure* and climbed out of bed to start the day. After I took a hot shower and slid on some clothes, I went over to Jay's place. I initially thought he was asking me over to cook, but to my surprise he wanted to go out to eat — his treat, he said.

It was a relatively cool day for a light jacket. The puffy clouds looked threatening, as if it was going to rain. We hopped into his black Acura and drove up the street to Boston Pizza. Once there we sat at a booth. A beautiful Indian waitress with a wall of luscious black hair cascading down her back came to our table and handed us menus. Jay and I ordered beers on tap to start. She

CONFUSED SPICE

left and came back with the beers. We decided to share a spicy pierogi pizza with smoked bacon, jalapenos, and sour cream. Jay was skeptical about the spicy part and asked for extra sour cream on the side. The waitress picked up our menus and tucked them underneath her arm. Before going away, she gave Jay a warm smile which he paid very little attention to while he took a sip of his beer. She strutted away with her vanity still intact. Once the waitress left, we sat in silence like two naughty bad boys in time-out. I sipped my beer, looking at the mosaic tabletop while Jay watched baseball on one of the many mounted televisions on the walls. The restaurant was half full with people dressed in business attire. My guess was they were on their lunch break from the small offices in the area. I wondered what made Jay bring me here.

"So, what's the special occasion?" I asked.

"What? Nothing yo. I just wanted us to do something different today." He took a long sip of his cold beer then gazed back at the television. The Blue Jays were playing some team I did not know. I pulled out my phone and started scrolling through pictures on Facebook, checking notifications on the pictures I'd posted last night in French class. I noticed Jay had liked all of them. I smiled to myself. I suddenly felt Jay's gaze directed toward me. I looked up.

"What kind of phone is that?" he asked.

"It's a Samsung."

"Does it take good pics?"

"It does a decent job. Why do you ask?"

"Let's take some selfies," he said with a bright smile. I wondered why he didn't want to use his phone, given it was a Galaxy. It was a lot more advanced than mine.

"Are you serious? You mean together?"

81

"Yeah, yo. Come on my side."

"The waitress should be back with our pizza in any moment, and you want to take pictures... Wouldn't it look strange? You don't care if she thinks we're gay or a couple or something?"

"Naw bruh. I don't care. That's her problem. Now stop wasting time and come sit next to me yo," he said, taking my phone into his beautiful slender hands. His fingers were long, with perfectly trimmed nails. I got up tentatively and looked around to see if anyone was looking at us. I slid into Jay's side of the booth, and he instantly placed his arm around my neck and started snapping selfies like a professional photographer, holding the camera at high and low angles. I couldn't help but laugh at his whimsical behavior. He took my aviator glasses off the table, placed them on his oval face, and pulled me closer to him as we took more pictures. The shades gave him a rugged look, especially with his three o'clock shadow. He radiated a sex appeal that sent a wild sensation through my manhood and body like a surge of electricity. He then took off my shades, picked up a bottle of Heinz ketchup, and pretended he was pouring it over my head while snapping pictures. I grabbed the mustard bottle and held it as if I was going to squirt some in his face. The camera clicked. The last picture was with our arms locked around one another's necks like best friends. If people stared at us in that moment, I didn't care, nor did Jay. We were in our own little world.

Our waitress, who was wearing a tight black t-shirt with a sassy slogan printed on the front that accentuated her breasts, came back to our table with the pizza. She looked at Jay and I as if we were a couple and smiled, and probably relieved that her beauty wasn't fading after Jay's earlier rejection. I unwrapped myself from Jay's warm embrace and slid back over to my side.

CONFUSED SPICE

He took the first slice of pizza, dipped it into the sour cream, and spoke while he chewed.

"So, what are you going to do with all those pics we took?" he asked with some words muffled.

"I don't know. What would you like me to do with them?" I asked, placing down my phone and taking a slice from the warm silver tray.

"Whatever you choose, yo," he said, taking a sip of his beer with a smirk.

Before taking a bite of my pizza, I posted a few pictures of us on Facebook and Instagram. Jay seemed to be witnessing this transaction as nonchalantly as possible. After hashtagging, I slid the phone in my pocket and bit into my pizza. It was still hot. I looked over at Jay. He seemed to be handling the spicy jalapenos pretty well. He looked content and gave me a winsome smile while chewing. After all, he got what he wanted.

13

Pierre

Jay had been silent for the past few days. I wondered what he was up to. I went online and logged onto Facebook. I noticed he'd liked all the pictures I posted of us at the restaurant. He commented on one picture with us in a tight embrace. He said, *Nice one bruh! We look good.* That made me feel some kind of way. I felt a smile spreading across my face. A tingling sensation touched the pit of my stomach. I imagined Jay actually saying those warm words. His smooth, energetic voice serenading my ears. I thought about replying to his comment but didn't know what to say, so instead I clicked the blue like button and closed my laptop. I rose from the sofa to get ready for French class. I thought it was best to eat something before going. That would prevent me from eating all those unhealthy yummy desserts. I toasted a plain bagel, slathered it with light cream cheese, and

CONFUSED SPICE

pulled out a store-bought fruit bowl from the fridge. After I finished eating, I threw on my coat and went out the door.

An hour later, I banged and beat the pastry dough on the wooden table with my rolling pin. My classmates looked at me as if I was a prime example of an angry black man that they heard so much about from the media and their xenophobic family members. I couldn't get the dough the way I wanted it and decided to chuck it and start over. The French instructor waltzed around the room, examining everyone's progress. Some students measured too much flour, some too much sugar, others way too much butter. She sauntered over to me and poked a finger into my newly prepared dough to see if it would leave a nice indentation, and it did. She looked at me with approval and walked on to the next student. I rolled out the dense dough into a square and kept overlapping it, lathering each layer with pure butter. I then sat it aside for a few minutes before placing it in the walk-in fridge to rest. I walked over to the stainless steel stove, where two Filipino students were cooking chocolate ganache. I watched a woman who looked like she was in her mid-thirties break chunks of dark chocolate into a silver bowl that sat on a pot of boiling water. Milk, sugar, and butter were added next. A few minutes later we were left with a silky smooth chocolate sauce that we would be using to pipe into the beignets.

The instructor slapped her chubby hands together and called the students to the middle of the classroom. We all gathered around her like a flock of hungry chickens in a coop. The instructor switched on a huge electric bowl mixer with a ginormous paddle hanging in the middle. I quickly grabbed my notebook from the communal workstation table and squeezed back into the tight circle. She went over the machine's functions. She pointed to me and asked me to get some eggs from the walk-in fridge. I

85

returned with several. She cracked each one with precision into the big mixing bowl and then added a few drops of vanilla extract imported from France. The class looked on as if she was the messiah of French cooking or Julia Child herself. I stood there watching her talk about the word "conglomerate" over and over. The word provoked giggles from the students and made them feel as if they were really in France in some fancy kitchen.

After class, I hung up my chocolate-stained apron and gathered my belongings in an adjacent room. As I made my way to the door, I paused at the long table hosting all the pudding tarts and chocolate-stuffed pastries that we'd made in class. I pondered taking some home for Jay. I dug through my backpack and pulled out a Tupperware bowl. As I raved the table, the most attractive guy in class came up and stood beside me.

"Lately, I've been making all my coworkers fat with all the high-cal desserts we've been making. They are loving and hating me at the moment. But hey, they're taking them with their own free will. It isn't like I'm giving it to them at gunpoint." He chuckled.

There's nothing more charming and attractive than a good-looking guy with a wicked sense of humor. I found him oddly attractive in a nerdy sort of way. He wore glasses and stood at five foot ten. He wore a grayish cardigan with a Kangol cap. "We haven't been properly introduced. My name is Scott, yours?"

"Pierre."

"Do you live in the area?"

"Over at McCowan and Progress."

"I always see you take the bus. Do you need a lift?"

I paused for a moment and then said, "No ... that won't be necessary. Thanks anyway." I shoved the last tart into my bowl and clicked it shut with a blue lid.

CONFUSED SPICE

"Are you sure? We're going the same way."

What am I doing? This is the reason why I don't have any gay friends in this godforsaken city. Besides, this doesn't have to be anything serious. He's only offering to take me home.

"On second thought, sure."

It was a breezy night. Fallen leaves crackled underneath our feet as we made our way to the parking lot. Scott pointed to his car where one lamp worked in the whole parking area. As we made our way toward his white Mazda, I heard honking from a distance and then my name called. I turned around. To my surprise it was Dre, my fiancé. Scott turned around and followed my gaze.

"Sorry, Scott, I totally forgot I was being picked up," I said, staring at him for a moment, and then back at Dre, who hung out of his red Maserati with a dazzling smile that lit up the dark night.

"No worries. I'll see you next week in class," Scott said with a half-hearted smile.

"Okay. See ya. Have a good night," I said before sliding into Dre's car, not wanting to create a scene.

"Hey, babe!" I sank into Dre's car without saying a word. "Were you ever going to return my calls?"

"Can we just go? I don't want to talk about it here." As we were pulling out of the parking lot, I saw Scott in my rear-view mirror standing there scrutinizing us as we drove off into the night.

I glanced at Dre and noticed he was dressed immaculately: black slacks, Armani shoes, and wearing a beautiful V-neck cashmere plum sweater that hugged his muscular arms like second skin. He hopped onto the 401, heading onto the Don Valley Parkway. "Where are we going?"

87

"There is a place I would like to take you."

"I'm not in the mood for one of your special surprises. I'm still dealing with the last one," I said testily.

He sucked in air and said, "Just wait and see. You'll like it."

I resumed silence while looking out the window, watching dots of bright lights from high-rise condominiums whip by.

Twenty minutes later, we pulled up to a high-end Italian restaurant called Buca. I remembered it getting five stars on DineTO. I started to protest the need to go home and change.

"Don't worry, sweet cakes." Dre reached into the back of the car and unearthed a black sports blazer with gray arm patches. As he handed it to me, I saw the label said *Massimo Dutti*. Our favorite store. Dre must've gotten it for me as a forgive-me gift. I placed it over my black V-neck shirt, and it fitted like a charm. I got out of the car, and Dre followed, tossing the car keys to a skinny valet guy dressed in all black, who looked like he was getting a hard-on over Dre's Maserati.

Before entering the restaurant, I noticed King Street was buzzing with activity. People were dressed up in their finest, and music was playing from every restaurant and bar on the stretch. Fluorescent orange lights installed on the ground led up to Buca. The restaurant was romantically tucked into an alley, making it feel exclusive. The ambience was incredible. Classical music was played as we strolled in, and big canvases of abstract-looking art hung along the cherry oak walls with grandiose see-through glass wine cellars.

A beautiful young brunette hostess wearing a sleek, tight black dress with her hair tied up in a smart bun stood at the podium with a welcoming smile. Dre gave her his name, and she quickly showed us to our table, which led me to believe we had a reservation. Once we sat, the waiter presented us with menus and filled our glasses with plummy red wine ordered by Dre. I picked mine up, took a whiff,

CONFUSED SPICE

and smelled notes of chocolate and smoky tobacco with undertones of fruit. We placed our orders, and then the waiter left us as quickly as he came. I took a sip from my glass and directed my eyes away from De'Andre to a lovely couple having a romantic dinner. I still wasn't in the mood to talk to Dre.

"Enough! Can we talk about this?"

"Sure we can, I'm all ears."

"I already told you I was sorry for what I've done."

"Are you really? In our bed, De'Andre? In our goddamn bed? And you think bringing me here will make me forget about all of it?"

"No, I don't expect you to forget, but I do want your forgiveness. I love you." He lightly pinkie-rubbed my finger across the table which induced me to gaze into his beautiful hazel eyes. I remembered when we first met six years ago back in Detroit. We met like most other gay couple meets: online. But this wasn't on some provocative website like Grindr or Scruff. We actually met by accident. One day I was at home checking email when all of a sudden I received an instant message saying *What's good?* I realized my best friend, Demarcus, had forgot to log out of his Yahoo instant messenger on my computer, which I let him use to look up used cars.

Instead of logging him out, I decided to respond so it wouldn't look rude on my best friend's behalf. I know how it felt to see someone online and say hello and then see them all of a sudden go offline without saying a word. That shit irritated me. So I wrote back explaining I was not Demarcus but his best friend. He sent me a message back: *Can we still talk?* I didn't see any harm in it. We ended up enjoying the conversation. He asked me out, and I accepted. When we got serious, he confessed that he was just coming out of a serious relationship with a woman,

89

which sent up red flags. But he was so sexy and intelligent that I wanted it to work. He said he wanted me, and only me. And that was all that mattered, even though he was attracted to both sexes. We hid our relationship behind closed doors because he didn't want his family to know about his sexuality, and he didn't want his close friends to know either. This led to arguments between us practically every day. But when Dre got a job offer in Toronto to work for CBC News, things became better between us. He was happy, and I knew this would be a great beginning for us. He popped the big question at dinner one evening at an expensive Italian restaurant in Detroit on Woodward Avenue called La Dolce Vita. That night, when he proposed, he promised things would be different since we were moving to a city that allowed gay marriages and was more accepting of gay culture. When we moved to Toronto, everything was going well until one day when I came home early from work and found him in bed with a Kim Kardashian look-alike. I couldn't believe it. Now he was sitting across from me, hoping that I would forgive him.

"Who was she?" I asked, pulling my hand away from his warm touch. The image of him thrusting his strong hips deep within her sex made my stomach turn ten times over. He leaned back in his chair and sucked in the air.

"She was an intern I was seeing before you came over to Canada. But you have to understand it just happened. She doesn't mean anything to me. I told her about us; my sexuality, but she refused to leave me alone."

"Oh yes, and she mistakenly fell on your well-endowed dick, right?" The waiter came with our entrees, caught wind of what I had said, and blushed and glanced at De'Andre, who flashed a cheeky smile with pride. I put down my glass with an audible thud, which startled the waiter who took that as his cue to leave.

CONFUSED SPICE

"So you're straight now?" I asked.

"No. I want to be with you only."

I took another sip of my wine to ease my nerves. He stared blankly at me, waiting for me to give him absolution. *Is this what I deserve for being with a bisexual DL man? Why do I always fall for these types of men?* Perhaps it was the manliness, the masculinity. Most gay men I met that were interested in me always turned out to be too feminine for my liking. If I wanted a female, I would date one. All of a sudden something caught De'Andre's attention behind me.

"Pierre?"

I turned around to the familiar voice.

"Vijay!"

"Who is this guy?" asked De'Andre, annoyed for being interrupted.

"This is my neighbor. He lives right across the hall." They stared at each other for a moment and then shook hands. De'Andre scrutinized him from the floor up, and I saw the muscles in his jaw tighten. Vijay looked sexy in a buttoned-up black shirt and tailored black slacks, standing tall. His hair was closely cut and neatly lined. It looked as if he had just jumped out of the barber's chair. And he smelled deliciously intoxicating with the scents of amber and leather.

"So ... Vijay, are you a busboy here?"

"De'Andre!" I shot him a look.

"Nah, bruh. I'm with fam."

"Your mother is here?" I asked.

"Yeah, man, she's right over there." I turned to see her adjusting a silver bracelet on her slender wrist, talking with a young woman I remembered seeing at their party. The Alicia Keys look-alike. Suhana wore a sleeveless skin-tight black dress, accentuated with a heavy pink grapefruit colored necklace. Her

91

hair was bone-straight and parted down the middle. I must say she was more beautiful than the last time I saw her. I wondered why she was there. I thought to ask Jay, who was staring at the table he just left. Before I could ask, Dre spoke.

"I'm sorry to interrupt you two, but I would like to enjoy my meal before it gets cold."

I shot Dre another look.

Vijay ignored him and spoke. "Yo Pierre, I'm going to meditation class tomorrow, would you like to come?" De'Andre's face tightened.

"Sure Jay. That sounds like fun."

"Great! I'll talk to you later. And you too, bruh."

De'Andre inhaled a sharp breath. "Is he gay?"

"No ... well ... I don't know," I said, trying to get under his skin. However, it was the truth.

The muscles in his broad jaws twitched as I poked playfully at my peas and carrots.

"Is he the reason why you haven't been answering my calls?"

"Oh! It's okay for you to cheat on me with some bimbo, but when I start making friends, it's an issue."

"Hey! Don't paint me as some kind of control freak."

"So what do you call this? Am I allowed to have friends? Or do I need to ask for your permission?" He sat back in his chair to restrain his anger and gazed at me as if trying to figure me out, like the colors on a Rubik's cube.

"Pierre, I'm not sharing you with anyone, understand that?" he said darkly. We fell silent and continued eating our meal.

Later that night, we didn't come to a resolution. Dre dropped me off and asked to come up. To get rid of him, I said I would call him tomorrow. I needed more time to think things through. De'Andre had been out of the apartment for over a month now.

CONFUSED SPICE

I didn't know where he stayed, perhaps at the Royal York hotel at CBC's expense, which they'd offered him for a year until he was settled in Toronto. Or he could be staying with that thot.

When I walked into the apartment, I wanted to call someone. I thought about calling my mother, and then I rejected the idea. She loved Dre like a son. He had always given her money whenever she ran into financial trouble where I was in no position to help. Telling her about our relationship problems would crush her heart, perhaps even more than mine. Calling my best friend, Demarcus, was an option, but he probably wouldn't give me any sound advice but instead tell me how dumb a bitch I was for moving to another country with a bisexual man who refused to tell his family about us. I wasn't in the mood for a lecture. So he was out. I sat on the sofa thinking over how I could've prevented this infidelity from happening. Perhaps I should've moved to Toronto when Dre asked me to. I thought it was a bad idea to move to another country without getting my Canadian Permanent Resident paperwork approved so I could work within the country, a process that took a year and a half. I could only imagine how lonely Dre must have felt. I was lonely too; however, I didn't go out and cheat. He was the one that jeopardized what we had. I had the right to be angry and hurt. But the question was, how could I pick up the pieces and move on?

I decided not to call anyone that night. I would work this out by myself. I don't need to worry anyone with my problems. This was my issue, not anyone else's. I plopped on the couch and thought about Vijay. It was great running into him tonight. My god he looked irresistibly hot all dressed up wearing a black tie. I wondered what was the special occasion. He probably would tell me the next time I see him. That reminds me, what to wear for this meditation class? Should I wear something fitted or loose?

MATHIS BAILEY

I have no idea. However, I'm glad he invited me. This invitation couldn't have come at the right time. I needed to clear my mind; to sort out this mess in my life.

14

Vijay

"So Suhana, darling, where do you work, and are you in school?" asked my mother.

"I'm still working toward my MBA at York University in Accounting, but I already got my BA in English."

"Oh, that's lovely dear. Did you hear that, Frank?" asked my mother, turning to Frank, who sat beside her, and then looked back at Suhana. "It would be nice to have an accountant in the family. But how do you survive living on York U campus? I cannot begin to tell you how many horror stories I hear and cases I deal with regarding young girls sexually assaulted while walking home from school near Finch Avenue. North York sounds like a dangerous area."

"Unfortunately, it is," said Mr. Minhas, smoothing out his brown tie and running a hand over his coppery hair with slight gingery streaks. He owned four Indian grocery stores in Toronto. "We didn't know about the problem when we moved there from Mississauga, but since this is our daughter's last year there, it doesn't make sense to move or transfer her. Besides, I pay for her to take jujitsu lessons on campus. Her idea," he said proudly.

"Yes. He's right," said Suhana, nibbling on a white asparagus spear. "You don't have to worry about this girl. I can take care of myself."

"Well, if you ever fall into any sketchy situation, I'm just a phone call away," said my mother, slicing into her grilled salmon drizzled with some kind of herb aioli sauce sitting on a bed of peppery arugula salad. The waiter saw that her glass was half empty and came over to replenish it with a bottle of San Pellegrino.

"What does your son do?" asked Mrs. Minhas, who was dressed in a deep purple sari with gold bangles on each arm. *Kum kum* was dusted down the middle of her hair, which symbolized her marriage. She looked like a traditional Indian wife who stayed home and made parathas and coriander chutney sandwiches all day.

"He's at U of T, studying Law and Political Science. Isn't that right, son?" my mother said, turning toward me with a proud smile. I sucked in a deep breath.

"Yeah, I'm finishing it up. Just taking a little break." I couldn't believe I'd agreed to be here. The Minhas looked like decent people. They looked at me as if they were sizing me up for a good sherwani. I looked over at Suhana, who gave me a slight wink. She was sexy for sure. Fair-skinned with long hair. I really didn't mind putting a ring on that. My mother actually had done a good job arranging this. But I still wasn't quite sure this what I wanted. I had my hand resting on the table and all of sudden I

CONFUSED SPICE

felt a soft hand on the top of mine. I looked to my right and met my nana's face. She gave me a warm smile.

"That's wonderful" said Mrs. Minhas. "I think you and my daughter will make an excellent match. And don't you worry about caste and horoscopes. We don't need all that done. We're not all that traditional. It's been challenging to find a good-looking boy for my Suhana. She is so picky. She refuses to be matched up with someone from my home village in India. I couldn't tell you how happy I was when you phoned me, Mrs. Morrison. I have good feelings about this union."

"That is great to hear," said Mrs. Morrison, smiling from ear to ear. "Shall we finish our meal before it gets too cold? I think everything has been settled."

The next day I decided to see my psychiatrist. I had some shit to get off my chest. As I lay on the IKEA sofa, I felt warm air from the vent making the room humid and stuffy. I loosened a few buttons on the top of my shirt and rolled up my sleeves. I looked at the doc as he got up, went over to a small side table near his desk, and poured both of us a cup of hot tea. He had on a pair of faded Levi jeans with a Bill Cosby-looking sweater. He handed me a cup and sat.

"It's been a long time, Vijay. What brings you here today?"

"My mother wants me to have an arranged marriage. I can't believe she wants me to go through with it. This shit is crazy," I said. Doctor McKenzie looked at me sideways and jotted something on his yellow pad. It had been roughly eight years since I saw my psychiatrist. I used to come to him for my depression. Shit that happened to me growing up in my childhood, like being bullied in school and home issues. My mother didn't know where all my anger was coming from, so she decided to take me to therapy, which was where she learned I was bullied for having the finer shit than my peers and also for being the only brown kid in my school where majority of classmates were white. My mother also used to be his client when she first immigrated to Canada, but I never learned the nature of her visits. The doc shifted in his cushioned seat.

"Why does your mother want you to have an arranged marriage?"

"She thinks it will help me grow the fuck up."

"Are you going along with this?"

"Yeah, I guess. The girl that she hooked me up with is fine as hell yo. I would be a complete dumbass not to get with that. She is every Indian man's dream: light skin, soft-spoken, long black hair, career-driven, speaks impeccable English. You know, the type of girl to bring home to moms and pops. She's far from being a Scarborough hoodrat and a thot."

"I beg your pardon? Hoodrat, thot?"

"A thot. Come on, Doc, you gotta keep up with me yo, I don't have time to explain these terms to you. A thot is basically a ho. A girl who craves meat often, if you catch my drift." I smirked at the doc as he nodded in understanding. "And a hoodrat is basically a ghetto chick with no manners."

"Okay. I understand. But why is a woman being light-skinned every Indian mans' dream?"

"An Indian woman being light-skinned shows how well off her family is in the Indian culture. Marrying a light-skinned woman will make me look good in the eyes of other Indians. But yeah, it's crazy yo. You have to be Indian to understand, Doc.

CONFUSED SPICE

But anyways. This whole arranged marriage thing got me fucked up. I still don't know if I'm going to go through it."

"If you don't?"

"Well, my mother is threating to cut off supporting my education and helping pay for my rent at my new place. I guess this wouldn't matter so much if I get two jobs." The doc jotted some more things down in his pad and rolled back one sleeve to read the time on his Fossil watch. A few seconds later, there was an abrupt knock at the door. The doc rose to answer it. It was his receptionist. She wanted to let him know that his one o'clock appointment had arrived. The doc looked at me, still holding the doorknob, and said, "We seem to have gone over our time. Is there anything else you would like to tell me before we end our session?"

I thought about Pierre. I really came to talk about Pierre. Should I tell the doc that my mother was a homophobe? Should I tell him how much I enjoyed Pierre's company? I looked up at the clock and said, "No, that was enough sharing for today. See ya, Doc."

I rose swiftly and strode out.

15

Pierre

*"Life is not measured by the number of breaths we take, but by
the moments that take our breath away."*

—Maya Angelou

$\mathcal{I}$t was six o'clock on a cold evening.
I rummaged through my closet for the skinniest jeans
possible for meditation class. I squeezed into my favorite
black H&M jeans that I wore the first night I spent with Vijay.
He seemed to like them, the way he was staring at me with those
smoldering dark eyes that night. I looked myself over in the
mirror behind the bedroom door. My ass looked nice. I tried
bending and stretching in them, and I thought they were uncomfortable. I flung them off and placed on some black sweats

CONFUSED SPICE

that made me look fat and bloated, but at least I was comfortable. I heard a knock at the door and thought it was Jay. I leaped to the door with a spring in my step.

"What are you doing here?"

"Is that how you greet your future fiancé?" I smacked my lips and returned to getting ready. "I guess you've forgotten I live here too," he said, closing the door behind him.

"I don't have time for this, Dre."

"Make time."

I turned around with my arms folded across my chest. "Okay, go ahead."

"I'm sorry for what happened." He had one arm behind his back and brought it before him. He was holding a fresh-baked apple pie from my favorite bakery, Wanda's Pie in the Sky. I couldn't resist one of Wanda's pies. I could smell the warm spices and the buttery crust perfuming the apartment. He gazed at me with his sexy hazelnut praline-colored eyes. As I was about to give in to this temptation, I heard a brisk knock at the door. Dre placed the pie on the kitchen counter and answered it out of old habit. Vijay was at the door wearing dark jeans and a beige trench coat, shouldering a Nike duffel bag. He was taken aback to see Dre.

"Yo, is Pierre in?"

"Hey, Jay!" I shouted over Dre's shoulder; he was blocking Jay from entering. I realized they were the same height. "Jay, I will need a sec. I'll meet you at your apartment." Vijay nodded and gave Dre a confused look before heading back to his apartment.

"I hope you're not going out with that punk-ass niggah."

"Who said he was black?"

Dre looked at me, befuddled. "What's his background?"

"That isn't important," I said. "He's a good friend."

"If he such a friend, how come he didn't invite me to come with you guys, your fiancé? Or you forgot to mention us?"

"He knows about us, and he probably thinks you don't like him. The way you treated him at the restaurant was despicable." He rolled his eyes. "Andre, you can stand here if you like, but we will have to continue this conversation later." All of sudden I had a suspicion that Dre was over because he remembered hearing I had plans with Jay. After I laced up my black Converse, I brushed passed Dre and closed the door without uttering another word.

I waited downstairs at the building entrance as Vijay pulled the car around to the front. He was blaring Jay Z's "99 Problems" and rapping the lyrics. His anthem, I assumed. He made a sharp turn on Progress Avenue, which caused me to lean hard against the car door.

"Yo, how come yo boy is always griming me like I owe him money or something?"

"He has?"

"Yeah yo, I don't think he like me much."

"No, that's not true. He said he likes you very much," I lied.

"He does?"

"Well, not in so many words, but I can tell he does," I said with a straight face. Vijay turned to me and gave me a sexy smile.

Once we reached uptown Toronto, we drove up to this seedy old building with a sign that that read *Tibetan Meditation Center*. The building was wedged between a Chinese takeout restaurant and an adult video store. We went around to the back of the building and found parking. Jay fed the parking meter and we made our way inside the building. We walked up the stairs and were greeted by a monk who wore a long red robe. His gray hair stood disheveled on top of his head, and his face was riddled with wrinkles and crow's feet around the eyes. He wore wire glasses and had a

CONFUSED SPICE

pasty, pale complexion. He shook Jay's hand and looked elated that he had brought a guest.

"Who do you have here?" he asked, taking my hand like a wise man from a faraway land. His touch was gentle and warm.

"This is my friend Pierre," said Jay.

The monk looked at me graciously and bowed his head. "I'm grateful that you could come." He turned to Vijay and told him that there was a meditation class already in session. He suggested that we should wait in the next room until the next one began. He escorted us to a room that hosted a long banquet table covered with a white linen tablecloth adorned with silver platters of assorted butter cookies accompanied by silver canisters of hot tea. There was another table littered with books by the Dalai Lama, Eckhart Tolle, and other spiritual teachers. The snack table beckoned me first, while the other drew Vijay's attention. After I finished at the snack table, I strolled over to Jay and handed him a cup of green tea. He thanked me, and I looked at the book he was holding: *Finding the Power within Yourself*. It had a young, good-looking Tibetan man on the cover wearing jeans and a crisp white shirt with a few buttons left undone on top.

The monk came back to the room and informed us a new session would soon commence. He saw the book in Vijay's hands and sauntered over.

"So, you want to become a Buddhist?"

"Very much so," Vijay said staunchly, like a young soldier ready to die for his country.

"Follow me, my son," the monk whispered. We followed him into a small room that had an array of colorful pillows strewn across the floor. The monk waved his ropey hand for us to have a seat. He sat on the floor with a practiced air, crossing his legs like a pretzel. I tried to follow suit but cursed myself for eating

MATHIS BAILEY

too many chocolate chip cookies just minutes ago at the snack table. I looked over at Vijay, who sat like he was a reincarnation of Siddhartha.

"So you both seek Buddhism?" asked the monk.

"Oh no, just my friend here," I blurted.

"You have a good friend to accompany you here, I see," said the monk. Vijay gave me a warm smile, which made me melt. "So, what do you two know about Buddhism?" He gave us a look as if he knew everything there was about the spiritual world.

"Buddhism is about realizing that the self doesn't actually exist and accepting suffering in order to transcend it," said Jay. The monk nodded, pleased with the answer. I was impressed that Vijay knew so much about Buddhism. His knowledge of this spiritual world made him seem more attractive and intriguing. I shifted around on the pillow, which was beginning to feel like a rock. Vijay kept his impeccable posture without moving an inch. How was he doing it? The monk noticed my shuffling and shifted his attention to me.

"Do you know anything about Buddhism, my son?" Vijay stared at me as if he wanted me to impress the monk, but I had nothing profound to say.

"Sorry, I don't," I said, not looking at Vijay who might've worn a disappointed expression.

"You know, I just came back from my trip to Tibet," said the monk.

This intrigued Vijay.

"How was it?"

The monk looked as if he had anticipated the question.

"It was a peaceful experience. It was very awakening."

"I wish to go someday."

104

CONFUSED SPICE

"You should, my son. But you don't have to go there to find peace. You can find it right here. Now, what I would like for you two to do is close your eyes." The monk slowly closed his eyes, and Vijay and I followed. "Take a deep breath. Feel your lungs expand with the air in the room. Take it in as far as your body will allow it to go, and then exhale. Be still and try to make a connection with the empty space within yourself. Try not to think of any images that may distract you from that space. Go deep until you find that quiet space within you. Don't think. Let your mind flow into nothingness, which will find calm. Take notice of your breathing. Feel the inner body. Be one with yourself. Cast away any negativity that may burden your mind. It's nothing but poison contaminating the spirit that prevents the light of enlightenment from taking place. Let the stress and worry melt away. Be still. Be aware of the sound of my voice. Hear the ticking of the clock mounted on the wall. Hear the faint sound of traffic outside this window. Be aware of silence."

After a few minutes, we opened our eyes. I felt nothing once again. I guess I was missing the point of this mediation thing. Vijay had a silly grin on his face like a madman. I could tell he was having way too much fun with this meditation experience. The monk motioned us to our feet. I stretched my limbs, letting the blood flow back.

The monk led us into a huge room with laminate flooring where people were walking in a circle in a reverent manner. Vijay and I slid off our shoes at the door and joined the circle with our heads bowed and hands clasped in prayer. I covertly took a glimpse of Vijay in front of me walking hard on the balls of his feet, making a slight thumping sound. He looked awkward, like a fish out of water. I could tell he was trying to mask his street strut. I looked around the room and saw pictures and statues of

105

figures I didn't recognize. In the middle of the room there was a shiny gold statue of Siddhartha.

After we walked a few more times in a circle, we sat on the polished floor. A woman with fiery red hair in front of me rocked back and forth as if conjuring spirits. A short-haired black woman next to me looked deep in thought and sat like a living statue. She looked near my age, in her late twenties. I saw her stare at me when we entered the room, perhaps thrilled to see a brotha joining her little community. An Asian man and a middle-aged white woman who had curly beach blonde hair walked into the room with gracious smiles. The room was silent. I coughed, which collected stares. Once the middle-aged woman started to speak, everyone focused their attention on her. I consulted my watch and saw that only twenty minutes had gone by since we been here. I gave a heavy sigh, which provoked another batch of stares. After the lady finished talking, the Asian guy took over and asked if anyone would like to make a donation to their non-organizational group. A few people got up and placed a few crumpled bills in the wicker basket. Vijay rose and donated as I stayed behind.

After the meditation session, a few people gathered in the snack room. I walked in and found Vijay in conversation with one of the monks. The black woman that had been sitting next to me came over to the snack table where I was eating a vanilla bean petit scone. She poured herself a cup of tea. As she poured, I noticed that the tea was milky white. She glanced my way and saw I was staring.

"Do you know what this is?"

"No, I don't, what is it?"

"It's buttermilk tea, it's quite delicious. Have some." She poured me some in a white Styrofoam cup. I took a sip. It tasted straight-up like melted butter. I tried to disguise my distaste for it.

CONFUSED SPICE

"You like?"

"It's alright," I lied, reluctant to take another sip.

"How long have you been a Buddhist?" she asked

"Oh, I'm not a Buddhist."

Her eyebrows furrowed. "You should become one; it has been the best thing that ever happened to me. It relieves the body of so much stress."

"How long have you've been practicing?" I asked.

"For two years."

A beautiful middle-aged white woman came up to us, kissed the black woman on the cheek, and introduced herself as Suzanna. She looked like the type that drinks kale juice for breakfast every morning. She now looked at me, waiting for me to introduce myself.

"Hi, I'm Pierre."

"I've never seen you here before."

"This is his first visit," said the black woman.

"Oh! How wonderful. Will you be coming back?"

"Um ... actually, I just came to support a friend."

"Who is your friend?" asked Suzanna.

"His name is Vijay, Vijay Khakwani." The ladies looked at each other with crinkled lines across their foreheads and then looked back at me. I pointed over to him.

"Oh, of course," exclaimed the black woman. "We met last week. Suzanna, you weren't here when he came." Suzanna looked disturbed at hearing this news, as though distressed that a newbie had slipped passed her detection. I set down the heart-attack-in-a-cup on the snack table and tried to make my way to the door. Right before I did, Suzanna asked a question.

"So where do you work?"

107

MATHIS BAILEY

The black woman leaned in as if she had been wondering the same question.

"I'm in retail."

"Are you married?"

"No."

"Do you live in the area? What's your background?" asked the black woman. I was beginning to think this was more of a pick-up joint than anything else ... and giving one look at the men here, I could see why I was receiving so much attention.

"I'm sorry ladies, but I must go. I think the time is up on the parking meter, and I don't want to get a ticket. Please excuse me."

As I made a beeline toward the door, I made sure Vijay saw me walk out.

He met me down below and still seemed excited that I had come with him tonight.

"Did you have fun?" he asked as we walked toward the car.

"To be honest, Jay, it wasn't my cup of tea. But I am glad that you enjoyed yourself."

"I did. I'll take it you won't be coming back with me anytime soon."

"I'm afraid not. Just isn't my scene. But thanks for inviting me."

"No problem, man, thanks for coming."

I started to laugh.

"What's so funny, yo?"

"The way you were walking in the circle."

"How was I walking?" he asked with his glossy eyebrows raised, which set against his dark cinnamon complexion in a seductive way.

"Nothing," I said with a dismissive wave.

"No, tell me." He smiled, now amused like a puppy being picked at a pet shop.

"The way you were stomping on the wooden floor with the balls of your feet, it was hilarious. It looked like you didn't know how to walk like the others."

He laughed. "I didn't, man. That was my first time seeing them do that yo."

"Oh, for real? I thought you'd been here before?"

"I have, but only to speak with one of the monks, the one you met earlier." He paused. "I've only spoken to him for a brief moment last week to get a feel for the place. And I also met this black woman named Christine. She suggested that I come back and give it a try."

"I think I've met her."

"Yeah, I know, she told me. She said she forgot to ask you for a donation. Do you want to give one?"

"No, not really."

"That's okay, I put enough in the basket for the both of us."

I smiled.

"Are you hungry?" he asked

I consulted my watch. It was a quarter past ten. I thought about making it a cooking night with Jay. I knew he wanted that, but the image of De'Andre came to mind. I forgot he was at the apartment waiting to talk about our relationship. He was probably on the couch watching *Property Brothers,* staring at the clock on the cable box and waiting for me to walk through the door any minute.

"Nah, I think I should get home."

Jay's face twisted a little, but he said, "Okay. Home it is."

MATHIS BAILEY

I turned the key in the door and saw Dre on the couch with his arms folded against his broad chest and his muscular legs suggestively open in grey sweat pants. He still had the same build as when he played college football at Michigan State. I closed the door, set the keys on the kitchen counter, and let out a deep breath.

"Did you have fun?" he asked with a little bit of sarcasm.

"Not as much fun you had with that thot," I quipped. Two could play at this game. I watched his face tighten.

"Let's not start now," he said resolutely. I raised my hands in surrender. "Come, sit next to me?" I kicked off my shoes at the door, came over to him, and sat on the opposite end of the couch. I smelled the fresh scent of shea butter body wash lingering on his skin. He must've taken a shower minutes before I came home. I looked at his clothes and noticed he had on a fitted black H&M T-shirt and sweat pants that gave me a generous view of his printed manhood. He took a swig from a bottle of beer he had sitting on the coffee table and gave me a dazzling smile.

"You're not staying here, Dre."

"I'm too tired to drive back to the hotel. It's all the way downtown."

"Sorry, Dre, but I still can't bear to look at you after what you have done. Do you have any idea how I feel?"

"Yes I do, and..."

"No, you don't. I can't even sleep in our own bed without thinking about what went down between those sheets. For the past month I've been sleeping here on the couch." He looked at me and ran a hand over his face, which was a yummy shade of butterscotch.

"Okay, I will buy us a new bed tomorrow."

"That's not going to solve anything."

"What do you want me to do?" he exclaimed, the veins in his neck becoming visible for a nanosecond.

"I don't know; I just need space."

"Babe, I can't stand being without you. I always think about you. I haven't contacted that woman since it happened. You must believe me."

"Did you have unprotected sex with her?" He looked at me and rose and took a deep breath. He slowly walked to the window with his hands linked on top of his head. I heard him take in another heavy breath. He stood peering out the window into the dark night.

"Yes, I did," he said, turning back to me. He looked at me with remorse in his beautiful hazel eyes that had rings of gold from the outside streetlights.

"You have to get tested. There's no telling what that filthy whore got."

"I actually already have."

"And?"

"I'm clean."

"Well ... that's good to know."

"Baby, I'm sorry," he said, coming over. He caressed the side of my face with his warm hand. The gentle touch made me surrender. I pulled him closer to me, wrapped my arms around his waist, and started to weep. I could tell he was crying, too, by the small teardrops falling on my head. I snuggled my nose in the crevices of his manhood, taking in the sweet scent. I untied the strings on his sweats and slid them down slowly until his sex flopped out. His manhood stared me in the face, saying "Hello." He was semi-erect, just the way I like it. I lifted it up with the warmth of my tongue and went to work. His sex became thicker and stronger in my mouth, filling every inch of space as I went back and forth. I felt him start to thrust. He tilted his head back in pure ecstasy. I noticed he had shaved off his pubic hair, and I liked it. The trimmed landscape made his sex appear even bigger. I heard him say my name in a hushed whisper as I grabbed his dimpled firm butt from behind. His groans grew louder. His massive arms hung listlessly at his sides as I slid my hand up his muscled chest, twisting and pinching his tight nipples. His balls knocked against my chin like a primal beast. They felt heavy and fill of cum. I sucked harder and faster as I moved my tongue along the side of his sex and back into my mouth, taking no prisoners. His mouth formed an "O." I began to taste his sweetness. He was getting close. He grabbed my head and took control. I began to make slurping noises as his thrusts became aggressive and violent. Once he climaxed, I felt the hot liquid smoothly go down my throat. I pulled back slowly from his sex and licked the last drops off my lips. He still had his head tilted back, relishing the moment.

As I slid up his sweats, he pulled me up onto my feet, held me against his broad chest, and said, "Your turn. "

For the past week, Dre had been spoiling me rotten by serving breakfast in bed wearing nothing but American Eagle boxer briefs with a gorgeous smile. This morning he had cooked me his special cheese omelet stuffed with caramelized onions and portabella mushrooms, accompanied by maple bacon and toasty focaccia bread. This month alone I had put on at least ten pounds from cooking class, my sessions with Jay, and now this.

After I finished breakfast, I climbed out of bed and went into the bathroom to splash warm water on my face to wake up.

CONFUSED SPICE

I noticed Dre was in the den working on an editorial piece for the *Huffington Post* regarding the Senate scandal. I gave him a cup of coffee and thought it best to head to the gym to start the day off right.

I went down to the recreational center in my building and slid the passkey into the gym's door, and a metallic beep followed. I walked in and saw a Chinese woman wearing a sweatband with yoga tights spinning like she was preparing for a marathon. She looked in my direction as if she was happy for a change of scenery. Her eyes followed me until I stepped onto the treadmill. Within minutes, sweat dripped down my face and back. I looked up at the flat screen TV mounted on the wall, and a commercial showing a good-looking guy running along the beach bearing his impeccable abs induced me to increase the levels on the machine. *I need to fit back into my skinny jeans, goddamn it!* No more looking like Aunt Jemima.

A half hour later, I saw my phone light up. Vijay's name flashed across the screen. It was unusual of him to call me. I answered it with exhaustion laced in my voice. "Hello."

"Hey, man. Sorry to bother you. Are you busy?"

"Not at all Jay, what's up?"

"Yo, I need a big favor."

"Anything." He told me his car had stopped on him coming off the 401. I told him Dre was over and that I would use his car to give him a jump. A few minutes later, I was at the location. He had a frustrated expression on his beautiful face while blowing on his hands for warmth. He saw me approaching in the snow and suddenly lit up with joy. I stepped outside the car, and the snowflakes stunned my cheeks. I took the cable cords out of Dre's Maserati and hooked them up to Jay's black Acura. After a couple of tries turning the engine, his car came to life. As we cautiously drove back on home in the thick snow, he rolled down the window and pumped his fist in the air as if I had saved the day.

We entered his apartment, exhilarated to be out of the cold. He asked me if I wanted some homemade soup. "My mother made it." He said.

After a grueling workout, I needed something hearty to regain my strength. He unclasped the lid on the Tupperware and divided the soup. When I took the first taste, I reckoned it needed salt and pepper. Vijay agreed and added some to his own. I noticed he preferred more spice in his food now as I watched him add a little cayenne too.

"It's really nice that your mother added barley and carrots to this. It's really tasty and nutritious. Just want I needed. Does she normally cook this healthy?"

"Yeah, man, she loves it. She called and told me she was making my favorite soup, and I was on my way in a flash," he said with a wide grin and then blew on the hot soup.

"Well ... this is delicious on a cold, snowy day like today."

I wanted to ask him a question, something I had to know.

"Vijay?"

"Yeah man, what's up?"

"What made you call me, out of all people?" This question caused him to stare at me with concentration.

"I had no other choice," he said simply.

"That's not true, Vijay. What about your stepfather?"

"I didn't want to disturb him. When I was at the house, he was taking a nap."

"Your mother?"

"You already know; I definitely didn't want to ask for her help. It would've just turned into a senseless shouting match.

CONFUSED SPICE

"Well, I'm glad you called." I smiled.

"Sorry if I interrupted whatever you were doing."

"Oh, I wasn't doing anything besides working out in our building's gym"

"Oh, for real yo?" Vijay seemed to like the sound of me keeping my body in order.

"Yeah, by the time you called I was already finished. So it was perfect timing. So don't feel bad."

I looked down and saw my soup was all gone. I placed the bowl on the kitchen counter and looked around the apartment, contemplating taking my leave. Dre was asleep when I left and was now probably wondering where I'd vanished to.

"Do you want more?" Vijay said obsequiously.

"No, I am full. Thanks."

"How are you and homeboy?" he said casually as he spooned himself another helping.

"We are doing better," I said honestly. I saw creases form between Vijay's glossy dark eyebrows.

"Really?"

"Yeah, we're doing actually okay now."

"It didn't look like it when I saw you two at Buca."

"We were actually in the midst of arguing that evening. He was trying to apologize for what he had done."

"What did homeboy do?" I took a deep breath, wondering if I should share my personal business with someone who knew little about gay relationships and gay culture.

"He cheated on me." When the words escaped my lips, I couldn't tell if Vijay was happy to hear this troubling fact in my life or concerned about my well-being. He dropped his spoon in his bowl, placed it in the sink, and went off into his bedroom without saying another word.

115

Seconds later, he emerged holding a red rose. It was a romantic sight. I didn't know what to think of the situation. He told me to come over to the dilapidated sofa as he took a seat. I sauntered over, confused, and took up residence close beside him.

"You see this red rose, Pierre?" he said as I nodded. "I don't think you do. I would like you to take it and examine it." He handed me the rose. The scent was strong and robust, as if it was just freshly plucked from a garden. "Now, I would like you to actually look at it," he said, sounding more neutral. "Just stare at the rose and tell me what you see."

I stared long and hard and didn't understand where Vijay was going with this. He bored his smoldering dark eyes into me as if I was a juicy slab of steak ready to be devoured. "Red petals?"

"No. Try again."

"I'm sorry, Vijay, but I don't know where you are going with this."

"You see," he said, turning more toward me with excitement. "The rose is almost like your life itself. You're going to experience some thorns along the way in life, but if you look beyond the thorns and into the design of the rose and into its core, you will find your way back home to the present moment if you decide to be still. That's where you will find peace and truth and happiness. Once you are still and centered, you'll know what to do next in your life."

I looked at him, amazed at this newfound knowledge. I stared at him as if he was another person. A person I had never met before. I liked this side of him, the calm, cool, collected side. He looked really sexy in these deep moments. "Where did you learn this technique?"

"From a book I've read. This guy I knew gave me this book called *The Monk Who Sold his Ferrari*. Good read."

"Oh, okay"

"The name of this technique is called The Heart of the Rose. It's a very effective method. You're supposed to stare at the center of the rose once a day for a few minutes to get rid of stress or any negative thoughts to restore balance in your life."

It was as if I was listening to a professional spiritual healer. This intellectual conversation made me even more attracted to Vijay. He was deeper than I thought. "You can keep the red rose, Pierre." He smiled. I twirled the rose in my hand smiling back and said:

"Thanks."

Vijay's cell rang, and he took the call in the other room. I looked at the rose and thought about everything that he had told me. I wasn't sure it would work, but I did like the fact he had given me a red rose. So romantic and sweet, even though he might have not meant it in that sort of way. But who cared. The gesture made me feel warm inside. I took another sniff of the rose and let its floral scent dance up my nose. I heard Vijay yelling on the phone in the other room. I assumed it was his mother. What could they be arguing about? Perhaps I should give him back the rose; it seemed as if he needed it more than I did. I stared at the door, contemplating leaving, afraid that I was overstaying my welcome. Right before I was going to leave, Vijay emerged from the bedroom with a book in his hand. I saw the title, *The Power of Now* by Eckhart Tolle.

"You can stay if you like, Pierre. I'm just going to do a little reading before I meditate. I would love to have some company." *What! He doesn't want me to leave? Yay!*

"Sure thing," I muttered. I checked my cell just in case I'd missed a text from Dre. Nothing. He must be still sleep or giving me temporary space. I didn't know what the hell I was going to do with myself while Vijay read.

As if reading my mind, he said, "You can use my Mac inside the room if you like, man. I don't mind at all."

"Great, I need to look up some recipes for our next cooking session."

When I strolled into his bedroom, it was in a bit of disarray. Clothes and different pairs of high-top sneakers were strewn across the beige-carpeted floor. I sat at the small desk in the corner and switched on the Macbook. I went to Allrecipes.com and looked at a few dishes. A stuffed Mexican pepper recipe looked delicious. I bookmarked it. Afterward, I browsed Facebook and YouTube. Minutes later, Vijay strolled quietly into the room with his nose buried in the book. He sat legs up in his bed against the headboard. I sensed he was staring at me from behind. Silence enveloped the room. I wanted to turn around and see what he was doing. Was he actually staring at me? I could feel his eyes burning behind my head, which sent a warm, tingling, sensation through my body. Was he admiring me from afar? Or could he be thinking about kicking this faggot out of his room?

I clicked on a Kanye West video featuring Nicki Minaj. I remembered Vijay talking about this video the other day and telling me to check it out. Not wanting to disturb him, I placed on the black Dr. Dre headphones that were lying on the desk. The video was sick and twisted. Nicki Minaj looked like a possessed demon like usual. After the video was over, I took off the headphones. The room was absolutely silent. No pages were being turned. I mustered the courage to turn around. Jay lay there listlessly with his eyes closed. Was he sleep? I stared at him for a long while. I could've sworn I saw his eyes twitch. He had on his usual basic black V-neck shirt and long NBA shorts with his hair freshly lined up. He looked handsome just sitting there. He slowly opened his eyes and met my gaze. I wanted to quickly

CONFUSED SPICE

turn away, but something prevented me. I felt awkward, but he did not.

"Were you asleep?" I asked, hoping his answer would be no, so I wouldn't have to leave.

"Not at all. I was just observing my thoughts."

"And what were those thoughts?" I prodded with burning curiosity.

"I can't tell you, yo," he said with mischief in his smile. Now I was extremely interested. I turned fully around toward him.

"Come on Vijay, tell."

"No, I can't say. It's very personal."

"You could share anything with me. Anything!"

He poked out his bottom lip in a shrewd way, as if weighing the pros and cons. "Nah ... nah ... I just can't yo," he said, shaking his head and sitting up straighter against the headboard. I was becoming a bit peeved at his reluctance to tell me what was on his mind. I wondered what he was hiding from me. I wonder if he wanted to touch me sexually as much as I wanted to touch him. I rose and moved onto the edge of the bed and shook his leg playfully.

"Come on," I implored.

"You just won't give up."

"Nope."

"I'm not telling you, bruh," he said resolutely. I could tell whatever he was holding back was something extremely personal. I could sense the heaviness of it. Something inside me wanted to press him more on the issue, but I decided against it.

"Do you like massages?" I asked, changing the subject.

"Yeah, why?"

"Come here," I said rather boldly. I didn't know what had gotten into me. He closed the book, placed it on the nightstand, and crawled toward me like a black panther stalking its prey.

119

MATHIS BAILEY

"Okay, I'm here," he said, looking up at me with those long-lashed dark eyes.

"Lie down."

He obliged, and I rose from the bed and got down on my knees. He slid closer to the edge so I could get better access to his body. I began to massage the sides of his temples in a circular motion. He closed his eyes to the sensation. I felt a bulge starting to form in my pants, and I wondered if Jay was experiencing the same throbbing feeling. I expanded my fingers more on his head. I could smell the sweet coconut hair oil that he uses, perfuming the room. My caresses became slow and sensual. Whispers of gentle groans escaped his perfectly sculpted lips. I felt my arousal fighting against the resistance of my trousers. I glanced down at his tall-framed body and saw his shirt hiked above his tight ass, showing off his dark blue boxers. I wondered if he was aware of the generous display. I kept massaging the key points on his head, as if I was a trained masseur. I could sense he was falling into a sweet lull. I could do this all night. The room became wrapped in a delicious silence. I looked over at the digital clock on the nightstand. It was after eleven at night. Where was I going with this? Touching him like this felt so right and so wrong on so many levels. I wondered if he was afraid to tell me to stop. "Do you want me to stop?" I whispered.

"Nah, man. This shit feels good." He groaned.

"You never had someone massage your head before?"

"Yeah, my ex-girl used to do this shit all the time," he said, balancing his head on his fist. I don't know why, but knowing that someone special already did this for him made me feel cheap. All of a sudden I started to feel pain in my knees against the hard, carpeted floor. I thought about shifting onto my hips but was afraid I would mess up the rhythm I had going. My eyes shifted

CONFUSED SPICE

back to his plum shaped-butt and was mesmerized by it. That was
another thing I wanted to touch and massage. Should I dare?

"So, Jay, are you ever going to tell me what was on your mind
earlier?" I cooed, trying to push the night in the direction I
wanted, but to my dismay it brought the night to a grinding halt.

"Man, I think that's enough," he said, opening his eyes, suddenly staring at me. "I'm getting tired."

"Okay," I said, rising to my feet and fighting the slight bulge
in my pants. I stood waiting for Vijay to walk me to the door as
usual, but he stayed lying down and groggily told me to see myself out. Why did he keep doing this to me? He was like Jekyll and
Hyde. One minute he was sweet as pie and the next he was being
a jackass. Why did I keep putting myself through this? I looked at
him one last time before exiting the room; he was now facing the
window, so I couldn't see his face. I walked to the front door and
left, leaving the red rose lying on the beaten-up sofa.

16

Vijay

"You should come to our weekly meetings at my home. You will learn so much about Buddhism."

Those words were said by the monk at the Meditation Center that Pierre and I attended a few weeks ago. I barely knew the guy, but I took him up on his offer. The thought being around authentic Tibetan monks exhilarated me. I wondered if Pierre would be down to go with me, given that he didn't care for the whole mediation thing. I sent him a text pretty much begging him to come. I explained to him the meeting would only be an hour, and there would be Tibetan food. The latter was the hook.

It was an unusually mild, sunny day in the middle of December. The sun was high in the sky and a light cold breeze brushed against my face as I strutted down Yonge Street toward Queen. I'd told Pierre to meet me inside McDonalds at the

CONFUSED SPICE

corner. I took a seat near the window and watched the people walk by, busy with their lives. A fine brown girl walked by and smiled at me. I thought about going after her and putting on Vijay Khakwani's charm, but I pulled back. I no longer misused sex. I want to avoid sexual pleasures at all cost. I thought it was the way of being an upright Buddhist. A way of living a better life without suffering. I pulled out one of the many books from my black Nike duffle bag and read until Pierre arrived.

"Hey. Vijay!"

"Yo Pierre, you're early, bruh."

"I thought to leave early. You know how Toronto's subway can be. You never know when a delay will pop up out of nowhere."

"Yeah, you're right. Hey! Since you're early, do you want to grab something to eat?"

"Naw, I'm okay. I grabbed a light lunch before I came."

Pierre stared at the book in my hands, trying to see what it was. Before he could, I stuffed it into my duffle bag and rose. "Do you mind if I get something to eat?" I pointed to the counter.

"Not at all."

I ordered a grilled chicken sandwich. The server tore my receipt from the printer and handed it to me with my order number printed at the bottom. I stood there waiting to be called while Pierre studied the menu. He had on form-fitting denim jeans and a blue V-neck sweater underneath his black trench coat. He was always put together. I wondered if he'd changed his mind about ordering something.

"Are you sure you don't want anything? It's on me."

"Well ... their new crispy chicken sandwich with sriracha sauce sounds pretty good. I guess I'll have that," said Pierre.

We ate our sandwiches on the streetcar as it screeched and jolted down Queen Street West. We hopped off at Spadina Avenue and strolled down a couple blocks to a Tibetan shop. I wanted to pick up some incense as an offering. A bell chimed as we entered the shop. A short, middle-aged Tibetan woman stood firmly behind the counter. As I browsed the dusty shelves, I noticed the woman staring attentively at us. The place smelled of sandalwood and burning ashes. Wooden prayer beads littered the cherry oak tables while Siddhartha statues dominated the narrow store, giving the atmosphere an ancient vibe. I picked up two boxes of incense that said *OM* and headed toward Pierre, who was staring at one of the beaded bracelets on a silver rack.

"You like it?" I asked.

"Yeah. It's really beautiful." He tried it on. The different shades of brown on the bracelet with a double-knotted black string looked sexy against Pierre's caramel complexion.

"Get it," I said.

"But I'm not Buddhist."

"You don't have to be a Buddhist to wear one. Besides, who would know it's a Mala anyway?"

"A *whatta*?"

"A Mala. It's used in prayer or meditation."

"Oh, gotcha."

We made our way to the shrewd-looking woman, paid for our purchases, and then headed down Queen Street. When we reached our destination, the area looked run-down, with windows cracked and clothes hanging on the balconies of dilapidated apartment buildings. I looked over to Pierre and could tell he'd never been to this part of town. I noticed the people sitting on porches and walking on the street were Tibetan. Pierre asked me how did I know their ethnicity. I told him it was from spending so much time with Tibetans since I started learning about Buddhism. They just had a certain look and a certain walk.

CONFUSED SPICE

But I was once like Pierre. I couldn't differentiate Tibetans from other Eastern Asians. As we were coming to the end of the block, I dug down into my pants pocket and consulted a piece of paper with the address on it.

We came upon a shabby-looking white apartment building. Two young kids ran around in puffy bright coats, chasing each other. Pierre and I entered the building, and I punched in a few numbers on the automated buzzer. A guy's voice came through the speaker. I said my name, and he buzzed us in. We waited in the lobby until a tall guy greeted us. He seemed to be around my age. He had on a crisp white shirt with a few buttons left undone at the top, wearing a pair of jeans and flip-flops. He looked pretty chill to be a Buddhist, I thought. We clambered into the small elevator and stood in silence. The elevator jolted and rattled as it ascended to the top floor. We entered the small apartment and were met by group of Tibetans. Pierre and I seemed to be the minority. All the men were cross-legged around a long table that was level with the floor. I wasn't sure if it even had legs, given that it was adorned by a white cloth that masked its nature. Women and children sat quietly at the side in chairs, some on the floor, I guessed due to the lack of chairs. We were gestured to sit in the circle by the chubby Tibetan monk at the head of the table. He wore a red robe. The men flanking him wore the same robe, and their bold heads gave them an air of wisdom.

After a few late comers trickled in, the meeting commenced. A young guy handed out a summary of subjects that would be discussed. The topics seemed philosophical: Reincarnation, World Environment, Theory of Relativity, and Quantum Science. *Shit! What can I add to this deep-ass conversation?* I look over to Pierre and watched the lines form across his forehead while he perused the itinerary. I shifted a little to get comfortable. I felt my hands getting clammy and cold. I can only imagine that Pierre wanted to strangle me for bringing him here. I hoped I wouldn't make a complete ass of myself. The monks spoke amongst themselves in accented English mingled with Tibetan. The physics that they spoke of went straight over my head, and I could tell over Pierre's as well. He was quiet and observing the ladies cooking in the kitchen. The place smelt of basmati rice and sweet milk.

Pierre looked as if he'd rather be in the kitchen with all the lively talking and the clanking of the pots and pans instead of here discussing physics and politics. One of the elderly ladies came from the kitchen and handed everyone a cup of hot butter tea. Pierre took a few sips, made a face, and set it down on the table. I could tell he wasn't fond of it. I took a long sip and noticed my tea was lukewarm. I guessed mine was the first one poured. I gulped the rest down and held the empty cup. The warm, milky substance soothed the tension in my stomach. I was no longer nervous but still remain noncommittal throughout the whole discussion.

When I realized the monks were more than capable carrying on the conversation amongst themselves, a certain amount of stress was taken off my chest. Occasionally the monks in the robes would ask the guests if they had any questions about the discussion. One of the women on the side raised her hand. Her questions were concerns about their Tibetan community, their living conditions, and their environment — things she was looking to do to improve her community. As she spoke, the monk who sat at the head of the table quietly listened while sitting with his hands rested on his knees. The light from the golden statue of Siddhartha behind him reflected off his shiny head, giving him a soft halo. He calmly uttered a few words that seemed to satisfy the woman.

CONFUSED SPICE

A few minutes later, the food came out from the small kitchen. I was handed a bowl of rice. I later learned from the monk next to me that it was a traditional Tibetan rice called *dresil*, which is only served on special occasions. The aroma of toasted cashews went up my nose. I spooned the rice into my mouth and tasted plump, sweet raisins that were soaked in butter. There was a spice in the dish that I couldn't put my finger on, which I assumed was native to Tibet. In the Indian culture there's a similar dish called pulao. My grandmother used to make it for me all the time when I was a young boy. Eating this conjured up some fond memories. I looked over, and Pierre had polished off his bowl before me. I smiled. I was glad he enjoyed it. Perhaps this trip wasn't a waste after all. A few seconds later, he leaned over and whispered in my ear, "Is there more food coming?" I shook my head, and he suddenly looked disappointed and bored.

After the meeting, the monks graciously shook our hands and thanked us for coming. Pierre and I headed out of the building. It was night, and we strolled in silence, not talking. I was really appreciative that Pierre had accompanied me to this meeting, and I hoped he knew that. I wished I could do something for him to show I was there for him during the rough patches of his relationship. Just to make up for all those times he was there for me. He was such a great guy. I playfully bumped into him, and he smiled and bumped me back. This day was a good day. Another day to remember. Another day with my boy. With my home skillet. With my ace. With Pierre Jackson.

17

Pierre

"Yes, I would like another cranberry orange mimosa," I said to the handsome black waiter taking my order. He had the most gorgeous toffee nut-colored complexion. He was tall and gangly, with sexy tats snaking up his lean, muscular arms. Seeing his veins bulging out of his arms made me think of sex. Before walking away with my order, he flashed me a gorgeous smile, which I reciprocated. After I watched him strut into the back of the restaurant, I consulted my watch; 12:30 p.m. I was meeting up with the Queen B: Octavia Brunswig, the executive producer at OMNI TV. We'd met at one of De'Andre's CBC colleagues' dinner party. She was a stunning woman, a mixture of German and Filipino. She'd recently moved from Victoria to Toronto for a new job. She was new to the big city, like myself, and was finding it hard to get around and meet new people. I instantly fell in love with her fashion sense. "Every girl needs a little black dress in her closet," she would say. I knew we would click like strawberries and cream. She was what you'd call a diva in every sense of the word, but she had the heart of a lamb if you really knew her.

She wanted to meet up for brunch at this French restaurant downtown between Wellington Street and Spadina Avenue for my coming up thirtieth birthday.

"Hey, sweetie!" she said, walking in. We smooched each other on the cheek.

"How are you?" she asked in a sing-song tone.

"I'm doing great."

She sat her white-and-gold Michael Kors purse on the booth next to her and pushed her Tom Ford shades up into her luscious black hair. "Did you order yet?"

"No, I haven't. I was waiting for you. I just ordered a cranberry orange mimosa."

"Oh, that sounds fabulous! I'll have one too." She snapped her manicured fingers at the waiter and placed in an order. It was the same waiter I'd been fawning over a few minutes ago. He brought me my drink, wrote down Octavia's order, and brought it minutes later.

"Isn't he fine?" I declared.

"Who?" Octavia spun around her head as if she was looking for Ryan Gosling himself.

"The waiter."

"Oh sweetie, Octavia doesn't do waiters," she said, snapping her fingers for emphasis.

"Well, excuse me, Miss Beyoncé," I said, laughing.

"You better know it." She sipped her plush pink mimosa. "So, how do you like the restaurant?"

MATHIS BAILEY

"It's very cute. I've never been here before. What's the name of it again?" I asked, scanning the restaurant and noticing Parisian pictures hung along the walls like an art gallery.

"Le Select Bistro. I wanted to bring you here, since you're interested in French cuisine. Perhaps you could blog about it."

"That's a great idea. I really need some new material for my food blog."

"How's your French cooking class going?"

"It's going great. I love it!"

"You know what, OMNI is looking for a food journalist to check out Indian restaurants and review them for our food segment. I told the producers that I knew someone who was a foodie and loves ethnic cuisine. They saw your blog and Facebook page with all the pictures of you in class and were impressed. So, is it something you would be interested in doing?"

"Of course. This sounds great! Wait until I tell Dre."

"I'm glad you're excited, hun," she said, showcasing her dazzling smile.

"Will I be on camera or writing these reviews?"

"Both."

"It's been a long time since I been on camera. I haven't done it since college. So I might be a little rusty. But writing isn't a problem."

"You will be fine, and besides, everything is pre-recorded, not live. Everyone always messes up badly in their first couple of months. Just write and practice your script, and you will be good to go. That's the only sound advice I can give."

"I really appreciate this."

"No prob, hun." We clinked glasses and took a sip.

"Thanks for bringing me here. I really do like this place. It's very French." She wore a smug look as if patting herself on the

CONFUSED SPICE

back for her good judgment and palmed her phone. A different waiter came back to our table with a basket of freshly baked warm baguettes. I tore off a piece of the soft bread and dipped it in olive oil. I passed a piece to Octavia, and she put up a hand. She skimmed through the menu and thought to have the watercress salad with poached egg on top and returned to her phone.

"Oh! Octavia, I have something for you." Octavia looked up from her phone in confusion.

"Here you are" I handed her a Christmas bag with Santa on it.

"Hun, you shouldn't have. It's your birthday, not mine." She rummaged through the colorful paper and unearthed a bottle of Chanel perfume.

"Oh gosh! Thanks. You are too sweet."

"No problem. I thought since this is your first Christmas away from home, I would get you something nice." I watched her face warm up.

"You really shouldn't have, but thanks. Oh my god, look who's here," she said, placing the gift beside her.

"Sorry I'm late."

"Trish! What are you doing here?"

"You know I couldn't miss your special day."

"But it isn't until next week."

"I wanted to give you an early surprise." Trish Walker was another good friend of mine I met through Octavia. She was one of those girls who needed no make-up — she woke up looking like Julia Roberts. She was a nutritionist and had graduated at the top of her class at the University of Toronto. She worked for clients in the entertainment industry. She unraveled the cream oatmeal-colored scarf from around her neck and took a seat next to Octavia. "Sorry for being a little bit late. I was stuck in traffic.

There was so much construction on the Gardiner," she said in her raspy voice.

"No worries," Octavia said, barely looking up from her phone. I felt a tap on my shoulder, and I turned around.

"Hey, bitches!"

"Daphne!" I exclaimed. Trish and Octavia beamed with delight. I guess everyone was in on the surprise.

"You girls are full of surprises," I said. Daphne took up residence next to me and ordered a cup of coffee with two raw brown sugars and cream on the side. She was Octavia's colleague and worked on *Bollywood Boulevard* as one of the producers at OMNI. We'd all hung out before, and Daphne and I instantly clicked. She took off her leather coat and she was wearing a flirty red dress. "Lovely dress, Daphne, but can you breathe?"

"Pierre, you know I wear push-up bras to give that illusion that you guys like."

"Too much information."

"Well, you brought it up."

"Yeah, I know, don't remind me."

"Would you like to give the girls a squeeze, birthday boy?" She grinned salaciously, showing her pearly whites. She was wearing a beautiful shade of red lipstick.

"No thanks, that is Giovanni's department." He was the Italian boyfriend she dated off and on.

"Oh, these girls haven't been receiving any action from him," she said, sadly poking out her painted lips and pushing her breasts together with Betty Boo eyes.

"Okay, guys, you two are a mess," Octavia chimed in. Daphne and I looked at her and back at each other, and we started to laugh. A waitress took our orders, and Octavia ordered her watercress salad with poached egg. Trish ordered the same. Daphne had the spicy lamb sliders, and I went for the rabbit linguine.

"Speaking of breasts, I almost had surgery for breast implants," said Trish as we all begun to take a sip of our drinks and looked at each other in astonishment.

"Really?" I croaked.

"Yeah. I feel my babies are too small. I think women with big breasts are more attractive."

"No way. Your boobs are just fine. They are like perky apples," I said.

"Exactly," Daphne added, sticking out her little bee stings in competition with the other ladies.

"How would you pay for something like that anyway?" I asked.

"Well, when I was paying for school, I used to know this older guy who was a regular customer at this bar I used to work at called Joe's. He was a generous tipper and enjoyed our small talk. He was pretty wealthy. From his tips alone I saved up enough money to think about going through the process."

"Why didn't you go through with it?"

"Last-minute jitters, I guess."

I looked over to Octavia, and sensed something was troubling her.

"Is everything okay, Octavia?" I asked.

"I think my roommate is upset with me because I told her I will be moving out by the end of the month."

"Well, Octavia, it is the last week of the month; don't you think that's kind of short notice?"

"Yes, but I found a wonderful apartment overlooking the Harbourfront with two bedrooms, two baths, and a walk-in closet that is the size of Mariah Carey's, and a vanity mirror to die

MATHIS BAILEY

for. It was an offer I couldn't refuse. Now my roommate has been giving me the silent treatment."

"When does your lease expire?" I asked.

"Within another month, but I'm moving anyway."

"Well, to give it to you straight, Octavia, if I were your roommate I would be upset too. I mean, who's going to help her pay for next month's rent? It's probably going to be difficult for her to find another roommate on such short notice living in the downtown core."

"She will be okay. Someone will snatch up that place in a heartbeat." The waitress came back and set our food on the table. I tried Daphne's lamb sliders, and they tasted bland. She agreed and sprinkled on some salt and pepper. My phone buzzed with a text: *How about dinner tonight? What you sayin yo?* Daphne eyed me suspiciously.

"So, Pierre, how is your love life?" she probed.

"Okay."

"Whatever. You've been missing in action for the past few months. The Indian Goddess inside me tells me you are seeing someone." Daphne was always able to see right through my bluff.

"Well ... it's this guy in my apartment complex. He's pretty good-looking."

"I knew it!" Daphne exclaimed then took another juicy bite of her burger. Octavia sat up straighter and placed down her phone, finally looking interested.

"Yes. I have met this guy. We've been seeing a lot of each other lately."

"What does he do for a living?" Octavia quizzed.

"Forget that, what does he look like?" Daphne quizzed.

"He's tall, dark, and handsome." Octavia heard "dark" and resumed back to her phone. She had the Asian white men syndrome.

"He sounds hot," Daphne said, urging me to go on.

"Well, he's Indian, but not gay. I think."

"Indian! Well, pass him over to me," Daphne joked.

"How quickly we forget Giovanni," I teased. He was a handsome Italian man whose voice could serenade anything in sight. She had a huge thing for him but wanted to act like he didn't mean anything to her. And he was one of those guys who didn't want a committed relationship. Daphne wanted more, however she never said this out loud, but I knew she did.

"What I'm saying is he is always blowing up my phone. I've been teaching him how to cook, and these sessions have become very frequent. Like tonight, he wants me to come over for dinner."

"But what about De'Andre?" asked Octavia. She'd asked the million-dollar question.

"We're still working some things out." I hadn't told them about the affair, but I decided to let them fill in the blanks. They only knew we had a disagreement.

"Well, Pierre, I think he's bi-curious," chimed in Trish, sounding cocksure.

"Who, De'Andre?" I asked.

"No, silly, the Indian guy."

"Why'd you say that?"

"How often does he send you messages?"

"Quite often, at least one message every other day."

"And the meeting arrangements have always been at his place, correct?"

MATHIS BAILEY

"Yeah."

"I believe this goes way beyond cooking. I actually think he misses your company and wants you near him every chance he gets." Everyone was silent, listening to the words spewing from Trish's pink lips. She placed a strand of hair behind her ear and continued. "This is what you should do if you really want to find out if he's into men..." We all leaned in with our elbows on the table. "Get him drunk."

"Drunk? I can't do that. That's like me taking advantage of him. I won't do it."

Trish popped a cherry tomato into her mouth and sat back in her seat. "Alright, it's all up to you. I'm telling you, it works like a charm. I can't begin to tell you how many interesting confessions have come out of guys' mouths when they had a few."

"How do I know what he says will be the truth anyway?"

"Honey, his mind might go numb, but his heart and dick will be pumping," Trish quipped, sipping the last drop of her mimosa.

"I'm not even sure he drinks."

"Well, find out."

I looked around the table, and everyone seemed to be on Team Trish. Should I do it? How would I go about getting Vijay drunk? Lately he's been all in this Buddhism thing. Perhaps I could use my birthday as an excuse to let loose. Trish got up and said she had a two o'clock appointment with a client and had to take off. She pulled out two twenties and kissed everyone on the cheek before she left. Octavia said she should be going too since she had to be at work within another hour. She told me she would have one of the producers get in touch with me about the details of when they wanted me to jump on board with the network.

136

CONFUSED SPICE

After we all kissed and hugged outside the restaurant, we went our separate ways. I pulled out my cell phone and contemplated replying to Jay's text. Since Dre and I were sort of back together, I'd been spending less time with Jay. Every time he sent me a text, I would tell him I was stuck at work or busy running errands. It was hard rejecting his texts. But I wanted my relationship with Dre to really work without outside interference. I stuffed the phone back into my pocket and turned onto Front Street.

"De'Andre Harris is getting ready for a conference meeting, but if you have a seat in the lobby I will tell him you're here," said a gorgeous black woman wearing studded diamond earrings and a fiery red blouse tucked into a grayish black pencil skirt looking as if she was Olivia Pope herself.

Since I was downtown, I decided to stop by the CBC to tell De'Andre the good news about my new gig at OMNI. I looked around the spacious building at all the offices and cubicles. A few moments later, De'Andre appeared, looking handsome in his well-tailored blue suit with a checkered maroon shirt underneath. As he got closer, I could smell the Tom Ford Vanilla Tobacco cologne that I got him for his thirty-fifth birthday. Since I worked at Saks, I got cologne at a very affordable price. He walked toward me with a serious expression.

"What are you doing here?" he said in a hushed whisper.

"I have some good news."

"Coming here was a bad idea, Pierre."

"Why?"

"You know why. I can't afford to lose this job," he said between clenched teeth.

"For being gay?"

"Keep your fuckin' voice down," he said, looking around to make sure no one was listening and catching the eyes of the receptionist, who looked at us suspiciously for a moment and went back to her work.

"Dre, I'm sure your colleagues will be fine with you being who you are. I'm pretty sure they have a discrimination code of conduct here."

"That's not the point. Look, can we talk about this later, at home?"

"But, it's really good news."

He sighed. "Okay, what is it?" He lightly tapped his leather chestnut-colored Cole Hann shoes against the polished marble floor. Right before I could get it out, a distinguished-looking older white guy came up to us.

"Mr. Harris."

"Mr. Chambers."

"We're about to start the meeting. You're anchoring at five, right?" the man said.

"Yes, I am."

"Okay, great. We have to get these stories lined up. Did you send out a video journalist to city hall? Rob Ford passed away. They holding a press conference there. We need b-roll for our five o'clock show before these smaller news stations beat us to the punch."

"I sent Sarah Louis." I wondered if that was the intern he was fucking. I looked around the building, pretending not to listen to their conversation.

"Great! She's a great reporter. I know she will bring back some sensational b-roll."

"Absolutely, that's why I chose her."

CONFUSED SPICE

"Excellent." Mr. Chambers looked me up and down with a Donald Trump strewed look before walking off.

"Listen, babe, I can't talk about this right now, I'm late for a meeting." He turned on his heels and jogged behind his boss. I stood there, once excited, now miserable. I decided to text Jay and told him dinner was on tonight.

"What! You got hired at OMNI?" exclaimed Vijay. I had decided to tell him the good news.

"Well ... not quite. I still have to go for an interview. But it sounds promising."

"That's great!" said Jay with a bright smile. "If hired, when do you start?"

"I don't know just yet."

"What will they have you do?"

"Reviewing restaurants around Toronto."

"That's awesome yo!"

"I know," I said with a weak smile.

"What's wrong, man?"

"Well ... cameras makes me nervous. I don't know how Dre does it every day."

"It's not that hard."

"What if I mess up or look terrible?"

"Wait! Where's my phone?"

"On the coffee table."

He grabbed it and switched it to camera mode.

"Talk."

"Huh?" I said, turning toward him on the sofa.

139

MATHIS BAILEY

"What's your name, and tell me about yourself." He looked at me intensely with those dark eyes, holding the phone close to my face as if he was a practiced cameraman.

"Hi, my name is Pierre Jackson. I am from Detroit, Michigan, where I was bought up and raised. My love is food, and I enjoy traveling the world discovering new cuisines and unique recipes so I can bring them to you and your family."

"Cut. Good yo. Just remember to take your time."

For a moment the room went silent.

"Would you like some tea? I bought this new tropical melon Lipton tea. It's pretty good," he said, getting up.

"When did you start being a fan of tea?"

"Ha! I just started. I learned drinking tea is the best drink to cleanse your body. So I need to cut down on coffee."

"Jay, you and these spiritual books."

"I know ... I enjoy them. So ... would you like some tea or what?"

"Alright, sure." He got up and strolled into the kitchen, pulling down two green IKEA cups. He returned to the sofa, handed me my cup of steaming hot tea, and said, "Wow, you working at OMNI as a food reporter. That is so cool. Let's cancel cooking plans tonight and go out to eat. Treat is on me yo. This news calls for a celebratory dinner.

I was glad I'd decided to come over Jay's place. He always seemed to know how to make me feel better.

＿ ＿

A few hours later, it was night. I sprayed on my best cologne and looked myself over in the bedroom mirror. I couldn't believe Jay

140

CONFUSED SPICE

was taking me out to dinner to celebrate my soon-to-be new job. He wasn't taking me anywhere extravagant, but I was still excited.

We arrived at Montana's a few minutes away from our apartment complex. We found a cozy booth in the corner with dim lighting. A pretty waitress took our order and came back a few minutes later with our steaks, mine medium rare and Jay's well done. The sight of pink freaked him out. I had him try a piece of my steak, and he spat it out after a few chews. I finally realized this was our first time actually going out to dinner. It felt great.

"Hey, I got you something." Jay handed me a heavy package wrapped in pink paper. "It's for getting the job."

"Oh Jay, this is so nice of you. But I didn't get it yet."

"You're going to get it," he said with that million-dollar-smile. I tore open the gift and read the title of the book. *The Book of Negroes* by Lawrence Hill. It was the special edition with illustrations. The book weighed as much as an encyclopedia. The smile on my face went flat. Did he give me this because I was black? I didn't know whether I should be offended or appreciative; after all, it was an award-winning book. "Thanks, Jay," I muttered.

"One day, when I came over to your place, I noticed you had really nice coffee table books. So I thought this book would be nice to add to your collection."

The books he saw were actually Dre's, mostly historical ones about prominent Canadian leaders like Mackenzie King and John A. MacDonald. I placed the heavy book beside me and resumed my meal. Before I took a bite of my juicy rib-eye steak, Jay interrupted.

"There's more in the package." He leaned forward with a grin, placing his bony elbows on the table. In the paper there were cooking magazines and an issue of GQ. I held the GQ magazine in my hands and stared at Jay, waiting for an explanation.

"I got you that because I think you dress so well. I think you will like the latest clothes in there, and they got a good amount of skinny jeans to look at. It seems to be their theme this season." He smiled.

So he noticed after all. Me in my skinny jeans. *Yes!*

"Thanks, Jay! This is more than what I could ask for." This generosity made me want Vijay even more. *Damn!*

18

Vijay

"What's up, Doc!" I said, entering the office and slapping him on the hand, which startled him. "What brings you here today?"

"My crazy mother again."

"Please have a seat." I took a seat on the long cream-colored sofa that was placed in the middle of the room. I reached and grabbed a handful of salted peanuts from a flower-shaped dish bowl that sat on the coffee table between me and the doc.

"Sorry for dropping by without making an appointment, Doc."

"No, no ... you are always welcome at any time." I'm pretty sure he meant that literally, given that my mother paid this joker three hundred dollars an hour. "Tell me what's on your mind," he said, taking out the infamous yellow pad.

"Well … it's my mother. She is driving me nuts, like that's something knew, right? But anyways, she is always butting into my personal life. Telling me what I should do with my life, my career, and who my friends should be and who I should marry. I mean, enough is enough."

"And what should you do with your life?"

"Bruh, I don't know. I'm still trying to figure that out, but I don't need her breathing down my fuckin' neck about it every second she gets. Don't get me wrong. I love my mother. I don't say it to her often like I should. But I do. She just needs to back off a bit. The one thing I know for sure is that I don't want to become a lawyer like her. I mean, that was my dream as a kid. But I think I was saying that just to please her. Just to feel accepted in her eyes, perhaps. Acknowledged. Now I have different plans, different avenues that I would like to explore."

"Have you voiced that to her?"

"She knows, but she doesn't care to hear about what I want to do with my life. She said everything I do is a waste of time."

"You said something about being accepted and acknowledged by your mother? Where do you think those feelings stem from?"

"Perhaps when my sister was born. I felt my mother finally had her perfect family. But I guess all elder siblings feel this way. Huh, Doc?"

"Is that all that's on your mind?" Dr. McKenzie crossed his skinny legs, showing his Mr. Rogers striped socks. I took a breath before asking the next question.

"My mother still wants me to have an arranged marriage. She believes that it will straighten me up."

"And how does that make you feel?"

"Like I'm not in control of my life."

"I see. Have you told her how you feel about it?"

CONFUSED SPICE

"Have I told her? Like my opinion matters. She doesn't care what I have to say."

"What else is bothering you?"

"She doesn't like one of my good friends," I said cautiously.

"And what is your friend's name?"

"Pierre. Pierre Jackson."

"Do you have any idea why your mother feels this way about Pierre?"

"Well ... he's gay." Once the words spilled from my lips like hot lava, I instantly looked at the doc's face to see if his stoic expression had altered, but what I said didn't seem to faze him.

"And do you think him being gay is the main reason she doesn't like him?"

"Well, perhaps because he might take an interest in me."

"And how does this make you feel?"

"I don't know. Good, I guess. But I'm not gay, though."

"I know. I know," said the doc, putting up his hand. "How often do you two spend time together?"

"Um ... almost every day."

"Do you think about him often?"

I paused, not sure how to answer this question. I looked at the clock ticking away against a sterile white wall. Should I tell him about how I read Pierre's old text messages repeatedly? Or how many times I replayed the videos I took of him on my phone, stumbling over his words? And how I laughed at his cute mistakes?

"Not much," I managed to say.

"Have you ever had sexual thoughts about Pierre?"

"Yooo, doc, I told you I'm not gay," I said, sitting up straight.

"Relax, Vijay. This is all a part of the process."

I rose off the sofa, towering over the doc as he sat back relaxed in his armchair.

145

MATHIS BAILEY

"I have to go. Charge the bill to my mother," I said, heading toward the door, not looking back. I heard him call out my name, but I kept walkin', not breaking my stride. This doc got me fucked up.

19

Pierre

A few days had gone by, and I still hadn't heard from OMNI TV. I finally told De'Andre about the new opportunity with the network, and he didn't seem impressed. He told me that was where journalist rejects worked if they couldn't land a position with the CBC or another major network. But he thought it was a great place to get my foot in the door. I didn't care one way or the other. It beat working at a department store folding clothes all day.

The day was winding down and I decided to take a shower. I let the warm water hit my face and neck and stood underneath it for a few minutes before jumping out. I toweled myself dry and sprayed AXE body spray on my chest and underneath my arms.

I walked into the bedroom and threw on a white T-shirt and a pair of comfortable pajama bottoms. I went to the kitchen and poured a glass of ruby red grapefruit juice before switching on the laptop. I checked Facebook for all the newest updates from family and friends. I noticed I had twenty likes, all from Vijay. A smile spread across my face. He also commented on one of my pictures of me dipping stuffed chocolate beignets into caramelized sugar. My right hand was sticky of the stuff. We were making *Croquembouche*, which was a traditional French wedding cake. We used the caramelized sugar as glue as we stacked one beignet on top of another into a shape of the Eiffel Tower. Once we were finished, the French instructor clapped her stubby hands for all the students to gather around. She placed three long rectangular baking pans on the floor, dipped a small whisk into a coppery bowl filled with warm caramelized sugar. She then quickly zig zagged a design onto the baking pans, creating thin wispy strings. Once cooled, she gently placed it onto the cake like a golden crown. The finished presentation dazzled the class. A few oohs and aahs escaped from students' lips. It looked too good to eat. I liked Vijay's comment before opening up my Gmail account. I read through a couple of junk messages, which I deleted. Then I saw a message from OMNI. Excitement ran though me. I opened it.

> *Hi Pierre,*
>
> *My name is Michael Shaw. I am the executive producer at OMNI. I received a reference letter from one of our producers, Octavia Brunswig, who told me you are interested in working in our food and travel department. I would like for you to come in for an interview, lets make it for next Thursday at 10 a.m.*
>
> *If you have any further questions, please feel free to shoot me a message.*
>
> *Michael Shaw Director/Executive Producer at OMNI TV*

CONFUSED SPICE

I couldn't contain my excitement after reading the email. I read it four times before closing my laptop. I wanted to celebrate, even though I didn't have the job just yet. I reached for my phone on the coffee table next to a *Toronto Life* magazine and called Dre. It rang a few times before going straight to voicemail. I listened to his deep on-air voice and left a message. I thought about who else I could call to share this joyous moment, and my mother popped into my mind. I made the call, and she picked up on the second ring.

"Hey, baby."

"Hi, Mom, I have great news."

"What is it, dear?"

"OMNI TV emailed me to come in for an interview. The job is reviewing restaurants around Toronto."

"That's great, dear. I hope you get it. Does that air in Detroit?"

"It's a network, and I don't think it does, but I will check."

"Okay. Let me know. Wait until I tell your brother and sister."

"How is everyone?" It was always a risky question; there was always some drama or other in my family about someone.

"Your brother is fine. He just brought a new house."

"Oh really?"

"Yeah, it's out there with those rich white folks in Farmington Hills." My brother, Germaine, was a fitness instructor and trained the most influential people in Detroit. I remember one of his clients was Judge Mathis. I could only imagine his job earned him a decent living, but he was always good with his money. Always saving every penny. He was the kind of person that would take a bus to work if the gas prices were too high.

MATHIS BAILEY

"Did you talk to your sister?"

"No, I didn't. How come?" I asked, sensing a problem that would kill my buzz.

"She's in jail."

"In jail?"

"Yes, dear."

"Why is she in jail?"

"For driving on a suspended license." I took a deep breath in frustration.

"How much will it cost to get her out?" My mother took a pause before answering. "Fifteen hundred?"

"What! What did she do, kill someone?"

"Well, when I called Oakland County, the officer told me she had a warrant for unpaid tickets as well."

"Oh lord." I expected this from a twenty-year-old, but my sister was turning forty. I had a savings account, but paying that amount would wipe me clean. I thought about asking Dre, but I thought it was unfair for him to always be bailing my family out of their troubles.

"Dre and I don't have that kind of money. Perhaps we could all chip in to get her out."

"I spoke to Germaine, and he said he didn't have anything to give after buying that house, you know."

"Oh, okay."

"But don't worry, dear. I'll have Albert go down there to straighten this out." Albert was my mother's special friend, who she didn't claim as her boyfriend.

"How did you guys come up with the money?" She giggled before answering. "Albert and I used a bit of our retirement money." Hearing this made me even angrier. But I knew my mother did it out of a mother's love for her children. But I also knew her

150

CONFUSED SPICE

generous giving would soon come back to bite me in the ass. I
did what Jay told me to do whenever I was upset: I took a breath.

"Well, at least she's going to get out," I said.

"That's right. The lord is good," she said.

"Well, Mom, I have to go. Keep me posted about that crazy
girl."

"Will do, dear. Oh! Before you go, let me wish my baby boy a
happy birthday."

I looked at the clock on the cable box. It was 12:00 a.m. I
totally forgot it was my birthday.

— —

The following evening, the Kennedy subway station was bustling
with people getting off work or out of school. Before catching
the bus home, I decided to order a vegetarian Jamaican patty at
a small coffee café. They are so good. As I stood in line behind
a young guy wearing a black and yellow Pokémon backpack, I
received a text from Jay asking me to come over. De'Andre was
working late, so I didn't see why not. Instead of texting him back,
I decided to call, something we rarely did since we'd met. He
picked up on the second ring, as if he was waiting for it. I wondered if he got excited whenever he saw my name flash across his
phone.

"YOOOO, Pierre, how is it going?"

"It's good, Jay, just getting off work from Saks," I said as I
mouthed spicy to a middle aged Indian man working behind the
counter. He had a thick black mustache and wore a no nonsense
expression. I watched him grab the silver tongs and place the
golden patty into a crisp white paper bag in a mundane fashion.

151

I paid him and took a bite of my piping hot patty while watching the steam escape into the cold air.

"Are you coming through?" I wonder if he had any idea today was my birthday. I'd mentioned it to him a couple weeks ago. But perhaps he forgot. However, I found it ironic that he decided to text me today after not hearing from him in almost a week since we last chilled.

"Well, Jay, today is actually my birthday."

"Your birthday! Oh man, that means we have to do it up big tonight." Oh wow, getting him drunk might be easier than what I thought. Now, what I needed to know was what kind of booze he liked.

"Great! I was actually heading to LCBO to pick up some liquor to celebrate my birthday and hearing back from OMNI."

"OMNI got back to you?"

"Yeah, the interview is next Thursday."

"You're going to knock it out."

"Thanks Jay. So, tell me... Would you like for me to pick up anything for you in particular at LCBO?" The phone went silent. "Hello?"

"Yeah man, I'm here. Um ... I usually don't drink."

I was going to ask how come, but this wasn't no time to be Oprah.

"Aw Jay, it's my b-day, you can't be a sober head on my special day." I knew he didn't want to let me down.

"Okay ... okay ... but pick me up some beer."

"Will do" I said, clicking off.

⌁ ⌁

Once I stepped off the elevator onto my floor, I heard soft music coming from Vijay's apartment. I noticed the music was seductive

CONFUSED SPICE

and slow. I pressed my ear against the door and didn't hear any voices. *Why do I keep doing this? I need help.* If I did hear a girl's voice on the other end, what would I do anyway? Storm in like a raging maniac and tell her to take her filthy pugs off my man? Just the thought of someone touching him propelled me to knock harder than usual.

"Yo Pierre, what's up?" he said, slapping my hand. "Come in," I placed the LCBO bag on the kitchen counter and scanned the apartment. He was alone. *Pierre, get a grip,* I told myself. I dug into the bag and pulled out a blue bottle of Alize. Vijay's eyes lit up like Diwali. I followed it up with a bottle of apple vodka. Vijay's face dimmed as if he saw the devil himself. He didn't say anything because he knew more was coming. Then I pulled out a bottle of tequila. Vijay's face darkened.

"YOOO ... Pierre. I can't drink this."

"How come?" I said shamelessly. For a moment he didn't say a word. He leaned his elbows on the countertop with the bottle of tequila cupped in his hands, looking at it as if he was studying its contents.

"Pierre," he said. "This stuff makes me horny as fuck." This sent hot, burning flames through my body. I felt soft oohs and aahs escape from my lips. He stared at me earnestly as if giving me a warning of which I needed to take heed. Excitement surged through me with utter and total abandon. Eroticism rose within me like never before. I looked him in his dark, piercing eyes and wondered why he was telling me this. Did he find me sexually attractive after all? I decided to push the envelope for information.

"What do you mean horny?"

"Man, I mean horny like fuck horny. So horny that I might even fuck the refrigerator," he said jokingly. He wore a black V-neck and Nike shorts. His dark skin had an amazing roasted hazelnut glow as if he sunbathed in the Caribbean sun.

153

"Okay, I'll tell you what, when you get that pissy drunk, I promise I will invite over my gorgeous lady friends."

"Really, bruh?"

"I'm gay, ain't I? We know a lot of beautiful bombshells." This seemed to put Vijay back in his macho state. We both knew I wasn't going to call any girls over, but I knew Vijay liked the idea, or needed some reassurance. He suddenly took notice of the shot glasses hooked on the tequila bottle.

"Yo, why do we have these?"

"It came with the bottle, and it was cheapest of the lot. So, will you be up for some Truth or Dare tonight?"

"*Ha!* That actually sounds like fun." I was happy that he was going along with everything. Now perhaps I would find out everything about Vijay Khakwani by the end of the night.

We went over to the battered sofa and sat all the booze on the coffee table in front of us. He twisted the cap off the Alize and poured us both a glass.

"So what happened to the beer?" *Shit! Think of something, Pierre.*

"I wanted us to have fun tonight, and we couldn't do that with beer."

"True. Oh! By the way, happy birthday," he said, raising his glass.

"Thanks." We clinked glasses and took a sip of the blue magic. It burned my throat as it went down. Vijay switched on Netflix and landed on a movie starring Denzel Washington. He scratched the idea of us cooking something special and ordered a large box of Domino's pizza. An hour went by, and I looked over at Jay from time to time to see if the blue magic had taken effect, but he seemed to be alert and awake. I picked at my slice of pizza, wishing the movie would hurry up and come to an end. This shit was boring as fuck. How many of these gangster movies

CONFUSED SPICE

Denzel was going to play? It seemed as if Vijay enjoyed these Mafia type movies, perhaps it evoked memories of his pass life as a hustler. I consulted my watch. It was one o'clock. The night was dwindling quickly. Vijay looked over at me, looking like he wanted to ask me something. The first bottle was completely finished. I felt him leaning toward me, and I straightened up, preparing for the moment. Oh sweet Geezus, was he actually going to kiss me? Perhaps the blue magic was working after all.

"Yo, are you going to have that last slice?" I looked down at the uneaten slice of pizza in front of me resting in the greased-stained box.

"No, you can have it." I handed it to him. A few minutes later, after there was no morsel of food left, I decided it was time to crack open the bottle of vodka. As I handed Jay his glass of vodka, he dozed off. I kicked him with my foot. "Jay! Wake up!" He jumped up as if he saw a ghost.

"What!"

"I know you're not going to sleep this early on my birthday."

"What time is it?"

"It's only one thirty," I said, trying to sound as wide awake as I possibly could. He sat up and rubbed his eyes while I switched on all the lights and powered off the TV. I felt this night wasn't going anywhere, so I decided to skip the vodka and bring out the heavy artillery. I grabbed the shot glasses and plopped onto the lumpy sofa.

"So, what now?" he asked.

"Ask me something," I said. He chewed his bottom lip in thought.

"Come on, Jay."

"Alright ... alright ... truth or dare?"

"Dare."

155

MATHIS BAILEY

"I dare you to go out into the hallway and knock on some-one's door."

That was too crazy. So, I took a shot. "Truth or dare?" I said.

"Truth."

I wondered if I should ask this question. What the hell.

"Do you masturbate? And if yes, how often?"

"You're asking me two questions, and besides, are you seriously asking me this, yo?"

"Drink or answer," I said with a smirk.

"Yes, I masturbate, but not as much. But I used to a lot though when I was in my teens"

"Oh, really?"

"Yeah, I was a horny boy back then. So horny that I used to hump this stuffed animal. I would jizz all over it almost every night." I twisted in my seat in excitement. I leaned forward for more of this filthy talk. I felt my nipples swelling and stiffening, screaming for Vijay's warm lips and teeth to tease them.

"Did you cum a lot?" I boldly asked.

"Yeah, man. A lot!" His beautiful eyebrows shot up at the last words. I didn't know where I was going with this, but I felt the tequila warming up my chest with a relaxing sensation. Vijay still hadn't taken a shot, but I could tell the blue magic was finally starting to do its job. He seemed awake and playful. I wanted to ask him if was he a shooter, but I sensed he wasn't that drunk, so I held off.

"Okay, your turn," I said.

He massaged his temples and snapped his slender fingers. "I dare you to dance for me for three minutes to any song of your choice." *What!* He wanted me to dance for him? What the hell? Besides, he forgot to give me a choice between truth or dare, but I guessed he was too smashed to realize it.

"Okay." I rose, strolled over to his CD collection, and ran my fingers across Lauryn Hill, Drake, Jay Z, and Rihanna. As I was still looking, I heard Jay unscrew the vodka. *Oh shit!* Is this actually happening? I found an Aaliyah album that I hadn't heard in a while and checked the track list. I knew the song that I wanted to dance to, and I slid the CD into the stereo. Aaliyah's sultry voice came through the speakers and filled the room with unadulterated romance. I turned around, facing Vijay, who held his eyes on the cherry-colored laminate floor, sipping his drink. "Rock the Boat" played as I began to roll my hips like a professional stripper. I dipped and twirled. He took another sip of his drink, stealing glances. I went over to him and stood between his long legs and started rolling my hips. I wanted him to want me, to desire me, to touch me, to taste me, to release his wild passion on me. He sat there stiff, nursing his drink, not sure how to react as I rolled my body to the music. Once the song came to an end, I sat back on the sofa with a thin layer of sweat glistening on my forehead.

"Okay it's my turn," I said as I caught my breath.

He sat up and looked more awake and alert.

"I dare you to take off your shirt." Without skipping a beat, he arched his back, sucking in his stomach while he lifted up his shirt over his head and flung it on the other side of the room as if it had been a nuisance to him all night. *Oh shit! What have I started?* I felt the temperature in the room rise on this cold wintery night. I didn't expect him to do it so willingly without protest. His body was hairless and blemish-free. The muscular definition in his arms and chest was too much for me to take in. I just wanted to reach out and touch the lines and curves on his gorgeous body. He stared at me as if he wanted me to do just that. He spoke breaking the silence.

"I guess it's my turn, eh?" he said. "I dare you to take yours off."

Oh shit! What did I get myself into? Once again he forgot to give me a choice between truth and dare. The rules of the game all of sudden went out the window. I tentatively peeled off my shirt, wishing I had shaved underneath my armpits this morning. I wondered if it would turn him on or off. We both sat there, shirtless. His piercing dark eyes studied my body from my shoulders down to my navel, making me feel a bit self-conscious. I realized this was his first time ever seeing me shirtless.

"What happened there?" He pointed to my stomach where there was a small scar. I looked down and touched it.

"I got it when I was a kid playing basketball in my friend's garage. It was filled with sharp tools. The doctor really didn't know what caused the cut but said I had come close to losing my life." He leaned over the confused space and traced his long fingers along the scar near my navel. His warm hand sent an electric shock wave through me.

"Were you in much pain?"

"Yeah, a lot; especially when I got stitches. The pain was excruciating." He drew his hand back slowly.

"How long did you have them in?"

"Probably a month or so. My mother was in hysterics when it happened. You should've seen her face when I came home wailing like a crazy person. She thought I had lost my mind and was ready to give me a good whack upside the head until she saw blood dripping from my hands. She immediately called 911. My mother held me in her arms until the ambulance arrived. She was really frightened. My father was at work, but came to the hospital as soon as he heard the news." When I finished telling the tale, Vijay had a weird look on his face, as if he was daydreaming. "What are you thinking about, Jay?"

"Mothers."

"Yeah, what would we do without them?"

"You seem very close to yours."

"I am, what about you?"

"Yeah, we are. In a weird sort of way, I guess," he said with a bit of a slur. He got up and went to retrieve something from his bedroom. It was a book. A book I remembered my cousin reading as a requirement in high school. It had three good-looking black men on the cover sitting on a staircase. They were all smiling. Jay handed me the book and asked me to read the message inside.

> *To my son, Vijay,*
> *I want nothing but the best for you. I read this book, and it is exceptional. I hope this book will inspire you to follow your dreams. Ever since you could walk, you told me how much you wanted to be a lawyer. And it's never too late to obtain that goal. I think this book will give you much guidance.*
> *Love Mom.*

I closed the book and handed it back to him. He rose and placed the book back where he got it. He came back with a catlike smile on his face.

"Why you have that look on your face?" I asked.

"What is the sexiest thing you've ever done for Dre?" I was wondering why he was suddenly bringing up Dre. I started to wonder if his buzz was evaporating. I pondered the question but was in no mood to air out our dirty laundry.

MATHIS BAILEY

"I don't know. What the sexiest thing you've done for your ex-girlfriend?" I deflected.

"I stripped for her on Valentine's Day and wore these black see-through fitted boxers with a red heart covering my piece." He smiled.

I tried to envision Vijay in these elusive boxers doing some exotic, enticing moves. My heart started to beat faster at the thought of him moving like a sex god.

"Do you still have these boxers?"

"I think I do," he said.

"Try them on. Let me see how you look in them."

"Sure. Give me a sec."

Is this guy serious? I couldn't believe he was going to put on some see-through draws for me. Could my poor heart take this un-adulterated eroticism? I felt my manhood rising in my pants. I tried to think of other things to take my mind off what was about to happen. Vijay emerged from the bedroom and said, "Sorry man, I couldn't find them."

I knew it was too good to be true.

"Do you mind if I listen to the radio?" He asked. I forgot Aaliyah's CD was still playing. I guess Jay wanted to listen to something less romantic.

"Sure."

He switched off the CD player and turned the radio to Hot 105.5 FM.

"Yo! This is my song," he said and starting to dance. I heard David Guetta come through the speakers. I also liked the song "Memories." This was what I loved about Jay; he was so spontaneous. He was like a drug that I couldn't kick. We danced around in the living room like two drunken sailors. Vijay had the bottle

160

of vodka in his hand, taking swigs from its neck like P. Diddy in a New York nightclub. He passed it to me, and I took a long swig. The room spun around us like a carousel. We fell onto the floor in pure exhaustion. Somehow, we ended up in his bedroom. We were huffing and puffing, breathless, with our shirtless bodies gleaming with sweat. His nipples looked like two Hersey kisses against his dark cinnamon complexion.

"I want to show you something," he said, rising to his feet. I followed. We stumbled into his bathroom bumping against the white wall. He opened up the medicine cabinet and pulled out a small spray. I took it from him and examined it. My vision was too distorted to read the label.

"What is it?" I said, swaying.

"It's a stimulant spray. It supposed to make you last longer in bed."

I stared at him in disbelief. Was this the reason why he didn't have a girlfriend? Was he a minute man? I felt a tickle rise in my throat. As soon as I knew it, I was bursting into laughter. Vijay's bottom lip pocked out in that shrewd way which provoked more laughter within me. I leaned against the wall for support. Tears began to roll down my face. All of a sudden, Vijay's posture became upright, as if his inebriated state had instantly evaporated.

"I'm getting tired, man. I think you should go." My laughter ceased like a hundred-year-old man's heart. I didn't want the night to be over, not yet, not now, not never. He brushed passed me before I could protest. He swung the front door open without meeting my gaze as I walked out. Before I could say goodnight, I heard the door click behind me.

The following morning, I awoke with a splitting headache. What happened last night? The only thing I could remember was the sex spray and being tossed out of Vijay's apartment. *Bastard!* All of sudden I felt my blood boil at the way he threw me out like a piece of trash. *Who in the hell does he think he is?* However, I was mad at myself for creating this predicament. I didn't know why I kept falling for bi-sexual men. They caused nothing but heartache and stress. I found it challenging to find a good-looking gay guy who didn't use the words "Girl" or "Bitch" in every sentence.

I crawled out of bed folding back the white duvet. I looked over to Dre's side of the bed and noticed he wasn't there. I looked at the digital clock on my nightstand. It was eleven o'clock. I figured he must be at work. Next to the clock there was a card and a box of Godiva chocolates. I opened the card and it read:

> *Hey snookums,*
> *Sorry that I couldn't celebrate your birthday with you. As you know, I got stuck at work. I was going to wake you this morning to give you your special gift (winks), but I thought I'd let you sleep. I figured you were hanging tough with Octavia and the girls last night. Well, enjoy the chocolates and happy birthday.*
> *Your poo bear,*
> *Dre*

I pulled the red ribbon from the golden box and plucked a white chocolate-covered strawberry from its tray. It was juicy and sweet. I sat the rest back on the nightstand. I rose and went into the bathroom to splash water on my face. I threw myself onto the couch and reached for my phone on the coffee table. I had three missed calls, all from Dre and nothing from Jay to apologize for his rude behavior. I sent Dre a text thanking him for the chocolates and sent a few flirtatious smilies. Then I got up and made some breakfast.

After I finished eating, I thought I should give Jay a call just to see if he was okay and not throwing up like crazy. But something prevented me from sending him a text. Moments later, I decided to call my best friend, Demarcus, in Atlanta, for advice. He picked up right away. He thought it would be a wise idea for me to send Jay a text. Once I clicked off with him, I sent Jay a couple of texts. I waited for a reply, but no response. I thought I would give him a few minutes to respond, and if I didn't hear back, I would call.

Meanwhile, I decided to take out the trash, and when I stepped into the hallway I heard music coming from Jay's apartment. He was playing Drake's song "Up All Night." I couldn't believe he was ignoring my messages. *Bastard!*

20

Vijay

Pierre was on my mind.

I walked around my apartment, not knowing what to do with myself. I'd been cleaning since I woke up, doing laundry and washing dishes. I needed something else to do to take my mind off last night. The thoughts I had about Pierre were outrageous. Was it the vodka? I didn't know. I just knew Pierre made me horny as fuck! He had my dick pulsating like an oversize artery. When Pierre left my place, I grabbed some St. Ives lotion and started to beat my shit. I could still smell Pierre's scent in the air. The thought of him made my dick wet. All naughty thoughts played in my head about the things that I would've done to him. I stroked my sex harder and faster. I tried to think about a sexy brown chick, but Pierre kept creeping back into my mind. *Damn, boy!* I moaned. I imagined him touching my

CONFUSED SPICE

dick, enjoying it growing in his hands. Then me flipping him over and biting his mushroom nipples with my teeth, just the way he would like it. *No!* This was wrong. My mind went to fucking Shima or Jessica. *Yeah, baby, what's my name?* I knocked the sheets on the floor as I spread my legs wider, stroking and stroking my manhood, getting wet and sticky. *Damn, this shit is good.* I relapsed back to Pierre. I was fucking him, slowly, pulling in and out, in and out. His ass was nice and fat and juicy, inviting me in like a dark tunnel for a speeding train. He wanted it as badly as I wanted him. I breathed his name into his ear as I plunged deeper. He moaned and scratched at the bed sheets as I dug deeper into him like a driller at work. He ground his ass against me, harder and deliciously. I liked it. I paused and enjoyed the sensation of his ass doing all the work. This was unfreakin' believable.

I flipped him over and fucked him missionary style, not slowing down the pace or the rhythms of our bodies smashing against each other like raging bulls. I could feel the temperature in the room getting warmer and muggy. He was thrusting his ass against my swollen dick as I fucked him, meeting him halfway. I was biting and twisting at his nipples. I licked and bit as he ran his hand through my hair, urging me to keep going.

His soft moans became louder and raspier. He jacked his dick as I fucked and licked and bit. I sensed he was close. I grabbed his arms and pinned them against the bed and whispered the words, "Not yet." Being inside him felt so good. I never thought I'd say it. Our bodies at this point were sweaty, and the air was enveloped with sex. I kissed his neck and chest, rolling my warm tongue up and down his smooth, delicious brown skin. He tasted so fuckin' good. I sucked and bit his bottom lip while he cupped my face in his hands in quivering pleasure. I inserted my long, slender fingers into the warmth of his ass, filling his hole as I

165

fucked. His soft moans morphed into strong groans. I felt warm, thick squirts hit the bottom of my stomach. I kept fucking, not missing a beat. I pressed my forehead against his and felt myself getting closer. My sweat dripped on his face, running down onto the white sheets. He sensed me getting closer too. Before I busted, he flipped me onto my back and licked and sucked my sex. This shit felt amazing. I grasped the edges of the bed as I shivered uncontrollably. I felt myself getting close. He placed all of me in his mouth, even my balls. I felt the blood rush through my body, as if I was about to explode. I could tell he wanted me to cum in his mouth, but I pulled it out. It went on my chest and cheek. From the look on Pierre's face I could tell he enjoyed the grand finale.

I lay there for a moment and slowly drifted back into reality. I opened my eyes in the darkness of my bedroom. Thoughts of tonight still played back in my mind, like a horror movie that I had no business watching. I leaned over on the side of the bed, grabbed a random shirt off the floor, wiped myself clean, and flung it God knows where and then fell back onto the bed in satisfaction. I looked over toward the nightstand; it was 5:00 a.m. I couldn't believe it was already morning. *Damn, I'm drunk.*

21

Pierre

The alarm went off at seven o'clock in the morning. My interview with OMNI wasn't until ten. I folded back the duvet and let out a fat yawn. I sluggishly strode into the bathroom and started brushing my teeth, followed up with a gargle of minty mouthwash. I switched on the shower and stepped into the tub, letting the hot water hit my face and back. Once I finished, I grabbed a big fluffy towel off the rack and dried myself and wrapped it around my waist as I sauntered back into the bedroom with beads of water trickling down my hairy legs.

I looked in my closet for a crisp white dress shirt and black slacks. I thought about wearing a tie for the interview but realized I didn't own any. I rummaged through Dre's array of ties and pulled out a burgundy and gray striped tie. After getting dressed, I checked myself over in the full-length mirror behind the bedroom door. When I walked into the living room, I heard the coffee pot bumbling and peculating. Dre was in the kitchen making himself breakfast wearing nothing but thigh-hugging white American Eagle boxer briefs which made his butt look like a perfect Georgia peach. He looked delicious. If I didn't have to leave within a few minutes, I would've had to get me some of that. He turned around and handed me a cup of hot coffee and strolled to the sofa to watch the morning news. First, Breakfast Television, CBC, then CNN. His morning ritual. I stood there in the kitchen with the coffee cupped in my hand watching the snowflakes fall outside. I sniffed the coffee before taking a sip. It smelled like his favorite blend: Italian roast. Dre always liked strong coffees, while I preferred flavored ones like French vanilla or hazelnut. After finishing my coffee, I gather my resume on the kitchen counter and gave Dre a kiss on the cheek before heading out. He wished me good luck and I was out the door.

An hour later, I was in the heart of downtown. I walked out of the subway station onto Yonge and Dundas. People dressed in heavy coats, black slacks, and penciled skirts milled the streets, nursing a warm-up cup of coffee from Starbucks and Tim Hortons. I checked my Google maps app for directions and noticed I was a few minutes away from my destination.

Once at the OMNI building, I went to the receptionist's desk to confirm my interview appointment with Michael Shaw. I was given a nametag pass with "OMNI" printed at the top. I clipped it onto my shirt pocket and was told to have a seat in one of the chairs against the wall. I sat back in my chair, feeling small. I looked back at the receptionist who looked as if she was nineteen. She was Indian, with an apricot complexion. She wore fuchsia lipstick and a yellow canary top with a knee-length light gray skirt. Her hair was fashioned up in a tight bun that said "I want to be taken seriously."

CONFUSED SPICE

As I sat, I watched the staff walk the halls, some carrying camera equipment and others hauling teleprompters, transporting them to studio sets. My heart leaped when I saw R&B/Pop singer Jay Sean. He was in deep conversation with Deejay Ra, an OMNI entertainment reporter. When I first met Vijay, all he would play was Jay Sean's hot single "Down." I thought it would be cool to ask for an autograph to give to Vijay, but right before I got a chance, Mr. Shaw called out my name.

"Mr. Jackson?"

"Yes," I said, standing up and giving Mr. Shaw a strong, firm handshake, which he reciprocated.

"It's good to meet you. Follow me to my office." He was Indian and tall with salt-and-pepper hair that contrasted becomingly with his gingerbread complexion. He was lean and in shape for an older guy. When we reached his office, I took a seat near the window overlooking the busy city and the Hard Rock Café. Mr. Shaw closed the door behind him and sat in front of me. I handed him my resume and cover letter, and he studied them with a shrewd eye. My palms began to sweat. My heart was beating twenty miles per hour. I felt as if I was going to pass out. But I managed to calm down by taking a deep breath, a technique that Vijay told me to do whenever I was upset or nervous. He said it will help me become centered.

"So, it says here you majored in Journalism."

"Yes, I did. I majored in journalism at University of Michigan. However, I didn't finish," I said, swallowing hard. Mr. Shaw looked at me in a pressing way and read more of my resume.

"How come you didn't finish?" he asked, not looking up.

"It was several things combined. My father fell ill, tuition ran out, and my fiancé received a job offer here in Canada ... so

169

MATHIS BAILEY

we relocated." I waited for Mr. Shaw to flinch at the fiancé part, but he didn't; instead he kept perusing my resume.

"What kind of experience do you have to work at OMNI?" he said, finally lowering my resume onto the table and lacing his long fingers. I noticed his nails were nicely trimmed.

"Well ... before I left college, I interned at a lifestyle magazine writing and editing for their food section and setting up interviews. I also run my own food blog, where I blog about new restaurants coming up around Toronto. So when I heard about this position, I jumped on it. It sounds totally up my alley." Mr. Shaw looked stern but pleased with my answer.

"How familiar are you with cameras and mics?"

"I would say pretty familiar. However, I wouldn't mind a refresher. It's been a while."

"Um, we might be able to help out with that," he said with a smile. "Can you start March 1?"

"Sure I can." That was a couple of months away.

"Great. We're still working on our food segment. Once we get everything up and running, I will have the director from the Food and Lifestyle department send you a call sheet of your first shoot. I also will have you train with someone for a week. Does that sound okay?"

"It sounds great." We shook hands, and I walked out the office feeling like I was floating on cloud nine.

"Stay away from my son."

The supreme high from getting the new job had instantly evaporated as I walked into my apartment. I wondered how this

CONFUSED SPICE

crazy bitch got my number. She must've gotten it off of Jay's phone while he wasn't looking.

"I beg your pardon, Mrs. Morrison?"

"Don't play coy with me. I know exactly what your intentions are with my son."

"I'm sorry, but I don't know what you're talking about."

"Ha! The hell you don't. Listen, I'm not the one to be taken lightly. My son is getting married, and I don't need you ruining his life."

What! *Jay is getting married?* Impossible. *Why didn't he tell me this?* But on the other hand, he hadn't known I was engaged either. I knew he was hiding a secret, but I didn't know this was it.

"I can assure you, Mrs. Morrison, that there is nothing going on between me and your son."

"There better not be," she said with venom in her tone. "Because you don't want me to expose your little anchor boyfriend, do you now?"

How did she know about Dre and me? Did Jay tell her? I'm pretty sure he was the source. However, I never told Jay what Dre did for a living. Since I'd known Jay I never knew him to watch the news. But probably once Mrs. Morrison heard the name, she did her research, checking social media sites, stalking our Facebook pages and putting two and two together. Besides, the CBC wouldn't fire Dre for being gay. The company was far too liberal to do such a thing.

"I don't know who you are referring to," I said, acting like I didn't have a clue.

"De'Andre Harris and his little play toy." The phone went silent. "Ha! I'm quite sure you do now. Heed this, stay away from my son! Or your big-shot boyfriend will be seeking employment at CP24." She hung up, leaving me listening to the dial tone. I sank back into the sofa, thinking over what to do. How did she know about Dre's affair? Did Jay tell her? But wait. How did she know about Dre fucking his intern? I hadn't told Jay that part. All of a sudden I felt responsible for Dre potentially losing his job. I also could see his dream job working at CNN shatter before my eyes. I thought about calling Jay and telling him what just happened. But I thought it wouldn't be a good idea. I didn't need to upset that wicked witch any further. Besides, I forgot we weren't on speaking terms. Perhaps our silent treatment was for the best. We needed to be apart.

22

Vijay

"We almost had sex."

I lay across the sofa with my hands locked behind my head. A stream of bright light from the window rested partially on my face as Dr. McKenzie jotted something in his yellow notepad. I looked at him sidelong to see if these words had startled him. But he remained cool and collected.

"What do you mean you two almost had sex? Are you referring to Pierre and yourself?"

"Yeah, Doc."

"I know the last time you were here, you were very touchy whenever I brought up Pierre. So the next question that I'm going to ask, you must remain calm. Bear in mind that all this is part of the process."

"I'm cool, Doc. it's just that you caught me off guard and shit. But shoot away."

"What made you almost have sex with Pierre?"

"We got pissy drunk on his birthday at my place. I always get horny whenever I have a few."

"Do you find Pierre attractive?"

"He's a good-looking guy. If he was straight, I'm pretty sure he could pull as many hoes as me." I lightly chuckled. But Doc didn't look amused.

"What kept you two from having sex?"

There was a moment of silence. I didn't know how to answer this fuckin' question. I shifted on the sofa and looked at the clock on the wall while listening to a bird chirp outside the window. I felt the doc's stare burning on my face as he awaited the answer.

"I told you, yo, I'm not gay. I don't play on that side of the fence. Liquor just makes my dick jumpy."

"Did Pierre make any moves on you? Or indicate he wanted to have sex?"

I pause for a minute. "I don't know. That's a good mother-fucking question, though."

"Perhaps he was just enjoying your company or hoped you would tell him more about yourself. Not all gay men want to have sex with their heterosexual friends."

"That's true, Doc."

"So what made you think he would have had sex with you?"

"Okay. I guess I should rephrase that. I almost had sex with him."

"What do you like about Pierre?"

"He's a cool-ass guy. Pierre isn't like any other guy I have ever hung around with. I feel like I can be myself around him. He has the ability to make me feel good about myself."

CONFUSED SPICE

"Have you ever had sexual thoughts about the same sex?"

I sat up and stared intensely at the Doc, as if he was a crooked cop out to get me. He looked at me strangely as I rose to walk to the window. The room was so quiet that I could hear soft voices from nearby offices in the communal building.

"I had sexual thoughts in the past about this one Indian guy I used to know in school. He was my tutor."

"What attracted you to him?"

"His body, I guess. I was young. He was young. Nothing happened," I said defensively.

"Would you think of yourself of being bisexual or thought of the possibility?"

"I love pussy yo."

"What did you think about when you thought about having sex with Pierre and this guy you went to school with?"

"Fucking them."

"Do you see yourself in a relationship with a guy?"

"No. I don't," I said, sitting back on the sofa. He asked me a few more questions, but my answers became clipped and short. He thought that was enough for today and that I was making great process. He suggested I keep a journal to record my thoughts. But fuck that. I didn't have time for it.

After leaving the therapy session, I felt better. I hadn't realize how much I needed somebody to talk to about these weird feelings. But now to have these thoughts out in the open, perhaps I could think about other important things instead of this gay shit. I wondered what was Pierre was up to. I thought about texting him but decided against it. I wondered had I come on to him that night? That night was such a blur. *Shit.* I felt as if something happened. Did I say something wrong? Did I say or do something offensive? No, of course I didn't. If I did, he wouldn't have

175

had texted me to see if I was okay after that night we got drunk. But now I didn't know how to behave with him. He probably thought I was gay and shit. He was probably getting the wrong fuckin' message. I hoped our friendship wasn't over because of some dumb shit I did. I really fucked up shit between us.

23

Pierre

The New Year was approaching, and I didn't want to start it off thinking about you know who. But his face always seemed to find its way back into my mind. I wondered what he was up to. I hadn't heard from him in weeks. I imagined him home alone reading a spiritual book on consciousness or something about living in the present moment. Or he could be at home getting it on with his bride-to-be, whoever she was.

My best friend, Demarcus, came to visit me for the holiday. Dre and I decided to take Demarcus downtown to see the gay life in Toronto. I thought about telling Dre about Mrs. Morrison's threat, but I thought I would bring it up once Demarcus was back on the plane to Atlanta. No need to spoil the weekend while he was here. Dre's colleague, Amir Sherazi, tagged along with us. He was the only guy at Dre's job who knew the nature of his sexuality. It all started when Dre spotted Amir in a gay bar called The Fly. Dre witnessed him getting his groove on with another man on the dance floor, kissing and all. Instead of fleeing the bar, I encouraged Dre to grab a drink with him, and he was glad he did. They'd been close buddies ever since.

When all four of us arrived on Church Street, we decided to go to this club called Woody's. The queue was out the door. When we got in, we found a table on the second floor where the crowd was thinner. Dre was a little apprehensive about venturing to gay part of town. I convinced him no one would recognize TV-polished De'Andre Harris in a fitted Yankees cap that covered half his face. I also told him that the partygoers would be too busy getting it 'in' on New Year's to concern themselves with scoping out a TV reporter. This seemed to put Dre at ease. He went to the bar with Amir to get drinks.

"Girrrl, he is fine!" said Demarcus, coming to the table with his drink already in hand. He was sipping on an apple martini. I followed my best friend's gaze across the room and looked at Dre's friend at the bar, talking to the bartender. He was tall with a creamy butter pecan complexion. I remember Dre telling me he was Iranian.

"You're right, Demarcus... he is fine. You should talk to him," I coaxed.

"Naw, chile. I'm not drunk enough to be so bold. But what's his name? He just makes me shiver all over." He did a little shimmy dance with his shoulders like Celie from *The Color Purple*.

"His name is Amir Sherazi. He's a video editor for the CBC."

"You need to hook up a brotha."

"Don't you get enough ass in Atlanta?" I poked.

"Chile, those gurls in Atlanta ain't nothing but trouble," he said, flourishing his drink in the air and taking a sip.

CONFUSED SPICE

"What do you mean? I thought the dating scene in Atlanta was poppin'."

"It is, but that's the problem: Too much eye candy. No one don't want to stay committed."

"So what are you saying? You're ready to settle down?"

"I think so ... a bitch is push'n thirty. Can you believe it?" I couldn't believe it; it seemed like just yesterday Demarcus and I were hitting up our first gay club when we were living in Detroit. Now those days were gone. We had that "been there, done that" attitude.

"I want someone who could love me and take care of me and look fine like your man De'Andre. Gurl, you really lucked up. I envy you. My heart is just as green as this apple martini, bitch." He rolled the eyes and took a sip. I looked over to De'Andre and examined how sexy he was. His intricate tattoos snaked up his muscular arms like an untamed python. Demarcus was right, I was pretty lucky to have a man like Dre. Even though he cheated on me once. However, I shouldn't let that diminish all the good times we've had.

"Here you are, babe," said De'Andre, handing me a chocolate martini dusted with salt around the rim.

"Damn, bitch, that looks good. I want one!" exclaimed Demarcus, ogling my drink.

"I'll get you one," said Amir, standing up with his Miller Lite in hand.

"Would you, darling? That would be so sweet of ya," Demarcus cooed, batting his eyelashes like a true damsel in distress. Demarcus wasn't a bad-looking guy, 5'9 with piercing grayish eyes. He could get any man wrapped around his finger. However, his relationships never lasted longer than a week. Guys would get fed up with Demarcus's overbearing, diva-like behavior.

179

MATHIS BAILEY

As Demarcus reached for his wallet, Amir put up a hand and said, "It's on me." Dre went along with Amir to the bar.

"Girl, I need to move to Toronto, chivalry is still alive up here," said Demarcus, staring at Amir in his skin-tight denim jeans that complimented his muscular thighs and butt. He looked like he could be in one of those steamy calendars of the world's sexiest men.

Rihanna's song came on "Please Don't Stop the Music" which galvanized the people on the dance floor. Blue and red lights flashed around the club, hitting every shirtless sweaty man. Young, lean, skinny white boys with green glow sticks danced around like go-go dancers trying to beckon in their New Year kiss. Everyone was feeling the music. I glanced over to Demarcus and sensed that he wanted to dance. Amir came back with Demarcus's drink and handed it to him. Demarcus tossed back the last drops of his apple martini and took up the new one. He nodded his head to the beat while taking sips of his chocolate martini.

"Amir, why don't you and Demarcus dance." Demarcus lit up like Golden Girls on Broadway. But Amir looked bothered by my suggestion.

"I'm not much of a dancer," he professed, looking more at me than at Demarcus.

"I'll teach you," said Demarcus, grabbing Amir by the hand and heading off to the dance floor. I noticed Demarcus left behind his chocolate martini barely untouched, and I placed my empty glass to the side and started sipping his.

"Do you want to dance, gumdrop?" asked Dre.

"No, I'm okay. I just want to sit here, if you don't mind." But in truth, I couldn't get Vijay out of my head. I missed him. I missed his smile, his jokes, and his playfulness. I just couldn't

180

CONFUSED SPICE

shake him off. I felt my phone vibrate in my pocket. The text read: *Happy New Year!* It was from Octavia. I texted back saying the same. I thought about sending a Happy New Year text to Vijay. But my ego wouldn't have it. I placed the phone back into my fitted jeans and took a long sip of my martini. A few seconds later, I received another text. It was from Vijay: *Hey man, I just wanted to wish you a Happy New Year.* My heart leaped out of my chest. I texted him back, saying the same. De'Andre eyed me suspiciously from across the table, witnessing the big smile on my face, of which I was totally oblivious to. I felt his stare so I looked up and told him I was receiving Happy New Year text messages from coworkers. This seemed to lessen his frown.

A few minutes later, Demarcus and Amir came back to the table glistening with sweat. Amir had his white T-shirt pulled behind his neck, showing the smooth black hairs on his broad chest. His face became more chiseled and intense like an Arabian prince. I wondered if Demarcus was going to spend the night over at his place tonight and thank me later for introducing them.

We ended the night with a round of tequila shots and stumbled onto Church Street. Partygoers were shouting "HAPPY NEW YEAR!" while kicking empty beer bottles and singing songs off-key. White girls walking the streets looked like Britney Spears' double wearing miniskirts and fishnet stockings while cars whizzed by honking in flirtation and celebration. I couldn't believe it was four o'clock in the morning and people were still having a good time. The air was cold and crisp, stinging my nose and cheeks. Amir had placed back on his Zara T-shirt and coat. He later locked hands with Demarcus. De'Andre and I walked behind in silence. No holding hands. No words passing between us. I wondered what he was thinking. I looked over at him and watched him blow smoke from his cigarette. When did he started back smoking? I had made him quit years ago when we first started dating. I felt I was losing him somehow, or we were losing each other in some way. With this revelation, I reached for his hand and held it tight.

We walked into a small takeout Middle Eastern restaurant called Ali Baba's to grab a bite to eat before hopping on the subway.

As I sat back in my seat on the train, I sank into a cloud of thoughts. I tried imagining Vijay and I together on this New Year's night, sitting on that beaten-up sofa in each other's embrace, sharing a passionate kiss. The kiss that he'd been dreaming about giving me since the day we met in the elevator, using this special night to surrender his true feelings for me. I sat there just thinking about the possibilities. Those sweet what-ifs. I could see myself ruffling through his spiky hair while his warm breath escaped down my neck. These thoughts floated around in my mind like feathers. But perhaps he wasn't thinking of me at all and was having a romantic night with his bride-to-be. Um, what was the name of that girl that he said he had a puppy crush on? I tried to remember her name, but it didn't come. "Oh yes, Tameka." If she was the lucky girl, I wished them both all the best.

The following morning, my head spun with a sharp pain from all the chocolate martinis I'd tossed back last night. It took me a minute to pull myself up in bed. As I swung my legs over the side, I heard muffled voices coming from the living room. I turned to De'Andre's side of the bed and noticed he was gone. He must be talking to Demarcus. As I stood up, I heard my phone vibrate on the nightstand. I reached for it and read *Come over. I will leave the door cracked.* Oh my god! I wanted so badly to put on my clothes and race right over to Vijay's place. It had been so long. It was a quarter past ten. I guessed he really did spend last night alone. I tried to think of an ingenious way to see Jay. I'd noticed that De'Andre always got jealous whenever I received a text from Vijay. He noticed the change in my demeanor, that bright smile sweeping across my face that he rarely got these days. But I just couldn't help it. I knew this neurotic love affair that I had with Vijay was ruining my relationship with Dre. But perhaps it was already ruined.

"Good morning, sleepyhead," said Demarcus as I strode into the living room. "I thought I had to come in there and pour cold water over you. A bitch needs to eat. Whatever happened to hospitality?"

"Well excuse me, I forgot I invited a southern belle to Toronto."

"That's right, bitch, and don't you forget it. NeNe Leakes is in the house."

I noticed De'Andre was staring out of the living room window talking on the phone which I assumed was one of his colleagues from the CBC. I didn't know why he was parading around the house wearing only pajama bottoms. Didn't he know we had company? I definitely would have to talk with him later about it. I suddenly thought about Vijay's text. *FUCK! I gotta find a way to sneak over there.*

"I'll be right back. I'm just going to take out the trash." Demarcus nodded as he flipped through a December issue of *Men's Health* that Jay had given me a few weeks ago. Dre was too immersed in his conversation to notice my getaway.

I dumped the trash down the chute and went over to Vijay's door. It was cracked, just like he said it would be, awaiting my entry. What to do? I stood in the hallway for a minute, contemplating my next move. I wanted to see him so badly. Just to see his beautiful face and the smooth outlines of his perfect lips. All of sudden I felt crappy for not spending time with him on New Year's eve, knowing the possibility that he was alone. I pushed the door open slowly and heard soft music playing. It was Alicia Keys' "Fallen." I felt my face getting warmer with each step I took.

"Yo Pierre, there you are. Look what I have for you." He was standing over the stove in a black wife-beater, showing his developed muscles. He spun around dividing scrambled eggs onto two white plates that hosted slices of oranges and apples, smoked sausages, homemade harsh browns, and buttered toast. His apartment smelled like he'd been cooking all morning.

"Vijay! You cooked all this ... for me?"

"Yeah, man, you taught me well. Try it yo, and tell me what you think," he said with a big grin. I forked a piece of sausage, along with the cheesy scrambled eggs. Vijay stared at me with beaming anticipation.

"This is delicious. What kind of cheese did you use in the eggs?"

"Smoked Gouda."

"Woah! Fancy."

He laughed. "I know you like the best."

"Yeah, I do," I said, eating some more.

"Come on. Sit. MTV is running a marathon of *Jersey Shore*."

I swallowed hard as he made his way to the dilapidated sofa with his drink and plate in hand.

"Vijay, I ... I can't stay."

He stopped in his tracks and turned around and stared at me as if I had told him I was having his illegitimate child. I saw

CONFUSED SPICE

the disappointment coloring his face, which he tried to mask. I wished I wasn't saying these words. But I was. I wished I could just make him happy and stay, but I knew I had to go back. Demarcus and De'Andre probably were wondering where I'd gone, or at least De'Andre was. He knew how long it took to dump the trash. Vijay sat his plate on the coffee table and sauntered toward me. Once we were face to face, I wanted to cup his face in my hands and tell him I would be back later. But I also knew that wouldn't happen. As he stood before me, I noticed he wore no socks. I always wondered what his feet looked like. I'd asked him one day when we were watching TV how come he always wore socks in the house. I knew it was an inane question, but I'd wondered what his feet looked like for some reason. He looked at me as if I had lost my mind and then asked if I had some kind of a foot fetish. I laughed and said "No," but deep down inside perhaps I did. Now Vijay stood before me barefoot with beautifully trimmed toenails. His toes were long and slender, like his hands.

"Heey! You're not wearing socks," I exclaimed.

"Yeah, just for you. I hate looking at them though."

"How come?"

"They're too bony," he said, staring down.

"They are nice." I smiled.

He looked up at me and smiled back. We locked eyes, and silence filled the room. I knew this was my cue to leave before I would say or do something that I might regret. As I turned to leave, he spoke.

"Well, at least take your food with you." He picked up the plate off the kitchen counter, looking at me as if he would be heartbroken if I didn't take it. I thought about asking him about his engagement but decided against it. I needed to get back.

185

"Thanks again, Vijay." I took the plate and slowly closed the door behind me while he stood planted motionless, overseeing my departure.

"Where did you go?" asked De'Andre with a slight edge in his voice. I was glad he finally had the decency to put on a shirt.

"I was over Vijay's place. I bumped into him in the hallway when I was taking out the trash."

"Is that a plate of food in your hand? If so, fork it over. A bitch is starvin'," said Demarcus.

"Oh, my neighbor made it. He had extra, so he gave me a plate." I handed the food over to Demarcus where he was sitting on the lazy boy like the Queen of Sheba.

He took a bite of the cheesy eggs and said, "This pass the smack-yo-momma test. Tell your neighbor he can cook for me anytime." He smacked his lips like a fat cow eating squashed cabbage leaves.

"Can I see you privately in the bedroom?" said De'Andre. I stared at him with concern and then back at Demarcus, who paid little heed as we went off to the bedroom. I felt a fight coming on, but as it turned out, I was wrong. "I can't go with you downtown today to show Demarcus around the city. I got a call from work, and they need me to anchor. Maybe I can meet up with you guys later for dinner." I told him that would be fine. He gave me a kiss on the cheek and headed toward the bathroom to take a shower.

CONFUSED SPICE

Demarcus and I got off at Union Station and took a cab to the CN Tower to have lunch. We took the elevator to the top-floor restaurant. A young, vibrant hostess sat us near a window with a panoramic view overlooking the city. The restaurant was nearly empty; I guessed everyone was still sleeping off their hangovers. A good-looking waiter came to our table, poured us each glass of water, took our order and left.

"Chile, I don't know about eating this far up. A bitch is scared of heights. But the view is gorgeous."

"And the food is just as great. I wrote about it on my food blog."

"I read it. It was nicely written."

"Thanks," I said, taking a sip of my water.

"I sure had fun last night. Amir is so hot."

"I was for sure you guys were going to take the romance back to his place. What happened?"

"Chile, believe me when I say I wanted to, but he wanted to take things slow. Can you believe that? A man turning down all of this?" he said, throwing up his hands like Diana Ross.

"Perhaps he wants something more than a fuck buddy."

"You think?"

"I think so; has he texted you today?"

"Yeah, chile, I was on his mind." He laughed.

"You should give him a chance. It's about time for you to try different flavors."

"Now, you know I prefer double chocolate chip over French vanilla any day," he said, glancing sideways at me.

"I know you do."

"So, how is everything with you and Mr. Man? How's the love life? The last time I spoke to you, you were crying like Angela Bassett in that Tina Turner movie."

187

"You know what happened?" I said, not really wanting to have this conversation. I finally was coming to peace with Dre's infidelity. I spoke to Demarcus about De'Andre's affair, but only in bits and pieces. I didn't give him a full, detailed story. I was too devastated and heartbroken to talk about it.

"Please refresh my memory."

"De'Andre cheated on me with some intern at his job."

"Shut yo mouth," Demarcus said, leaning forward. "What did you do?"

"What you think? I kicked his ass and tossed the bimbo out of our apartment."

"Did you give that bitch time to put on her clothes?"

"Nope."

"You are a cold heifer; remind me not to fuck with your man," he said, squeezing a slice of lime into his water and taking a sip. "So, is the wedding still on?"

"I think so ... we pretty much made up in our own sort of way."

"Why did Dre sleep with her?" Now he had asked the important question. De'Andre was bisexual, but he said he would give up women for me. But I knew he still had strong attractions to the ladies. I noticed how whenever we went out to the supermarket or to the movies he would stare salaciously at a sexy woman.

"I don't know why he did it. My guess is that he was lonely. The affair started before I moved here. But it's all under the bridge."

"Well ... chile, you are a good one, because if that was me, I would have karate chopped that hoe in the head and cut off his dick like Lorena Bobbitt."

"I'll bet you would have, but everything is fine now."

CONFUSED SPICE

"So, I guess that means I'm still making a trip up here this summer for you guys' wedding?"

"Yeah."

The food arrived minutes later, and the waiter set it on the table with grace. He gave Demarcus a flirtatious smile, which was reciprocated.

"Giiirl, did you see that?"

"Yeah, you both are tramps."

"Who you calling a tramp?"

"I call it when I see it," I teased.

"Whateva, but just to let you know, I'm coming up here to live. The men here are fine as hell." The waiter looked like he was a mixture of Native American, Asian, and black. He was very attractive. "So, tell me, who is this Vijay that I keep hearing about?" he said, cutting into his steak.

"Oh, he's this guy I have been teaching how to cook."

"It seems like every time I call you, you always headed over to his place. If I didn't know any better, I would think you two were fuckin'," he said, waggling his fork in my face.

"I don't know what's going on between us myself, to be honest."

"Is he gay?"

"No ... I mean, I don't think so."

"What do you mean you don't think so? It's either he is or isn't."

"Well ... I don't think he has come to terms with his sexuality yet, I will say that much."

"Bitch, are you trying to turn him?"

"No."

"You and these down-low straight men. Chile, they are nothing but trouble."

189

"But I think he thinks of me as more."

"What makes you think that?"

"I don't know ... it's just the things he says and the sweet things that he does."

"Um ... I see. Have you gotten him drunk yet? Because a good bottle of vodka will easily bring this mess to a conclusion," he said while chewing his food like a farm animal.

"I tried that. Nothing happened."

"What exactly went down?"

"Well, we got drunk at his place, and he showed me a spray that makes men last longer in bed."

"And...?" he said, chewing his food slowly with growing interest.

"I didn't know what to think of it, so I laughed at the situation."

"You dumb bitch," said Demarcus, throwing down his fork, which clanked against his white plate.

"I was drunk, okay!" I said, adjusting the white cloth on my lap.

Demarcus resumed eating and forked a wilted white asparagus into his mouth and continued. "You could've gotten yourself some good Taj Mahal dick." He shook his head at my blunder. "I believe he wanted to fuck you senseless."

"In a way I'm glad nothing happened. It seems like he is going through a lot, and I didn't want to add to the drama."

"Well ... you can play Mother Teresa all you want, but I know men, and it sounds like to me he wanted to get up in that ass," said Demarcus, leaning back in his cushioned chair, lifting his drink off the clothed table and crossing his skinny legs like Sasha Fierce, he continued, "Why do you think he showed you that sexual spray, so he could let you borrow it?" He giggled. "Chile, he had his eye on something else that night."

CONFUSED SPICE

"You don't know that for sure," I said.

Or was my naiveté getting the best of me?

━ ━

The next day, De'Andre and I drove Demarcus to Pearson airport and dropped him off at his terminal. I got out and gave him
a long hug. It was great having someone to talk to these pass couple of days and nice to have someone around to use as a sounding
board. De'Andre got the luggage from the trunk, trying to avoid
scratching the car and dirtying up his white cotton pants at the
same time. He took off his black shades and place them on his
head to give Demarcus a hug.

On our way back home, we drove in silence. I felt alone again.
No one really to talk to, and Vijay was back on my mind.

24

Vijay

"I cooked him breakfast, Doc, and he just left my apartment leaving me hangin' like a motherfuckin' joke. Can you believe that shit?" I said, sitting straight up on the stiff sofa with my elbows on my knees as Mr. McKenzie scribbled something illegibly in his yellow pad. I felt a light, cool breeze brush against the back of my neck from the slightly open window behind me, which soothed my anger a bit. "I never cooked for anyone before, not even burnt toast for my dumbass ex-girlfriend who shamelessly dumped me for another guy."

"What made you cook Pierre breakfast?"

"There are a couple of reasons. The first reason was I wanted to do something apologetic for tossing homeboy out of my apartment on his birthday. That wasn't cool after I looked back on it. Second, I just wanted to surprise him on what he taught me in

CONFUSED SPICE

the kitchen without him supervising a brutha. But that nigga didn't look like he appreciated it. I had to encourage homeboy to taste the food before he left."

"What was the reason for him leaving?"

"He was saying some shit about his best friend being in town for New Year's. But I know he was hurrying back to be with his cheating-ass fiancé, De'Andre."

"If that was true, why does that bother you so much?"

"Who said it was bothering me yo? I was just pissed off about the simple fact that homeboy left me hanging."

"But it sounds like to me he had a good reason for leaving."

"Yeah, whatever, Doc. I should've taken Suhana up on her offer to come over to my place on New Year's Eve that night to watch the ball on TV drop. Instead I told her I had plans the following morning."

"What were the plans?"

"Well ... cooking that niggah breakfast, for one. Like I said before, I haven't seen Pierre since that messed-up night on his birthday. So I thought cooking him breakfast would break the ice between us. Besides, I had some important news to tell him."

"What kind of important news?"

"That shit doesn't matter anymore, Doc," I said, waving a dismissive hand and strolling to the only window in the office, watching the congested traffic on Yonge Street. I turned back facing the doc and leaned against the eggshell-colored walls when McKenzie fired off the next question.

"Are you still marrying Suhana?"

"That shit is still up in the air, Doc. The whole arranged marriage thing still isn't sitting well with me. My mother is beside herself about it. She's already talking wedding arrangements with Suhana's mother. Shit is getting real yo."

193

MATHIS BAILEY

"So, are you going to go through with it?"

I fell silent as I directed my gaze toward the window and then down at my crossed ankles with my arms folded across my chest. I looked back up at the doc, who was staring at me with much anticipation. I broke the deafening silence and said, "I'm not sure."

25

Pierre

Four o'clock in the afternoon. I was at home sitting on the couch thinking about you know who. That intimate night at Jay's place on my birthday and that thoughtful day when he cooked me breakfast had me thinking about him like clockwork. I was wondering if he was thinking about me as much as I was thinking about him. I hadn't heard from Vijay for two days, which felt like weeks. Should I text him? I thought about his mother's ominous threat and soon vanished the idea. I wanted to see Vijay just to know he was okay about me leaving him alone on New Year's Day. The memory of him looking sad and disappointed made my heart sink. I reached for my phone on the coffee table and then lowered it to my lap. Perhaps I should give him his space. I kept reverting back to that salacious night of our shirtless bodies taunting the air with sex in his apartment. Maybe I should call him, or at least send him a text saying hi. I just wanted him to want me as much as I wanted him, nothing more, nothing less. I looked at my phone, wishing he would send me a message to pacify this insatiable hunger to hear his voice and to see his beautiful face. Every time I left my apartment, I would stand in the hallway motionless outside his door, trying to hear music or footsteps beyond it. Our distance was driving me crazy. I finally came to the decision to send him a text. If he didn't respond, I would definitely know for sure where we stood.

A few minutes later, my phone lit up. It was a text from Jay. My heart skipped a beat. All of a sudden I felt warm and gooey inside. *What does this boy have over me?* He'd texted me my favorite song, "We Need a Resolution" by Aaliyah. I wasn't sure if the text held any innuendos. All I knew was that it was a cute gesture to ease the tension between us. Another message followed asking me what I had plan for tonight, and I sent him a message back without wasting a nanosecond, saying *nothing.* I needed to see him. I needed to see Vijay Khakwani.

I knocked on Vijay's door. It was eleven at night. I waited until Dre went off to bed to sneak over Jay's place while I left the TV running in the living room. Jay answered and there was a moment of awkwardness between us. As I walked in there were big brown boxes everywhere.

"What's going on, Jay?"

"I'm moving." This was a shock to me. A sudden blow to my heart. I wondered if this had anything to do with that crazy night on my birthday. And perhaps he couldn't bear to look at me anymore. But what he said next extinguished those thoughts.

"The landlord has raised the rent on this place. I can't afford it any more. Besides, I lost my job at Foot Locker." He stared directly into my eyes.

"What about your mother? She could..."

"No, bruh! I'm not going to ask her for any more money."

"Where will you go?"

"I don't know yet, I'm still trying to figure that out. I've been looking, though."

I thought about him staying with me just until he found a place, but I knew De'Andre wouldn't have it. I looked at Vijay, and he met my gaze. He seemed really out on the ledge.

"Is there anything I can do? Do you nee..."

"No!" he said vehemently and then softened his tone. "I'll be fine."

"When do you need to be out?"

"Within a few days."

I looked at him, wanting desperately to help, and he sensed it and spoke. "You know what, I actually need to check for some apartments online. Do you mind if I use your computer?"

"What happened to your Mac?" He turned his head away and stuck out his bottom lip in that shrewd way.

"I sold it."

"What? Jay! When?"

"It doesn't matter. I didn't need that thing anyway. I'm becoming too materialistic. I believe things happen for a reason."

We went over to my apartment. All the lights were off when we entered. As we made our way into the study, I heard Dre snoring in the next room. *Thank you Jesus!* I exclaimed inwardly. I led Jay into the room where the laptop was sitting on a black desk. Within a few moments, the blue screen flickered to life and he started to type away. Condominiums popped up. I left the room to give him privacy.

When I came back, the laptop was switched off. He sat at the desk, staring at the black screen.

"Any luck?"

"Nah, nothing available that's affordable," he said, running his slender fingers through his hair. It had grown a few inches since the last time I saw him. It looked straight and soft. I wanted to touch it. "What do you use this room for?" he asked, looking around. It was equipped with a twin bed and a closet.

"We use it for Dre's office and for a guest room," I said apprehensively. I hoped he wasn't getting any crazy ideas. I heard De'Andre cough and rustling in the next room, and so did Vijay, who looked at me and realized that whatever he was thinking wouldn't work. I was relieved the question didn't come up. I wouldn't know what to say if he'd asked to stay here.

I walked him to the front door and felt like a lousy friend.

"Thanks for letting me use your computer."

"No problem."

There was confused space between us as we stood in the doorway. I was going to miss being over at his apartment laughing, cooking and staying up late. Now the days were counting down for us to part. And I knew he felt it, and so did I. He leaned against the white wall with his hands locked behind his back, staring into my eyes as if he was waiting for me to do or say something of any consequence or urgency. There was a heavy silence. If it weren't for my inner editor, I would've told him my true feelings, the heated passion that I held for him. How much I longed to hold him in my arms and tell him everything would be okay.

As he turned to leave, I quietly called out his name.

CONFUSED SPICE

He turned and looked at me. I extended my arms.

"You're a cool guy, Pierre, but I don't give hugs," he said, and left.

It was 4:00 p.m. Today was the day that Vijay was moving out.

I heard him moving back and forth from the elevator to his apartment carrying his belongings. I hadn't spoken to him since he left my apartment a few days ago. Perhaps it was for the best, so I wouldn't have to deal with his psychotic mother. I ignored all his text messages and sent all his calls to voicemail. I sat on the sofa wrapped up in De'Andre's arms watching *Love It or List It*. We were startled when we heard a crashing sound in the hallway.

"Oh, it's Vijay," I said nonchalantly with a dismissive wave.

"What in the hell is he doing out there?"

"He's moving."

I saw a faint smile spread across De'Andre's face. I didn't hear anyone else besides Vijay bustling about in the hallway. I thought for a moment to help him, but De'Andre's embrace had me glued to his broad chest, as if he was reading my thoughts. Then he all of sudden loosened his grip and asked, "Why aren't you helping your buddy?" I sensed he was prying now; curiosity killed the cat. Dre was gone, and De'Andre Harris suddenly appeared live on the scene.

"He didn't ask for it," I partially lied. Jay had sent me a text this morning telling me he would be moving out in the evening. And when I didn't respond to it, he came over that morning while De'Andre was at work. But I didn't answer the door. I was still upset with him for rejecting my affection. I felt he'd

199

MATHIS BAILEY

harpooned my heart and thrown it to the sharks. I couldn't believe how damaged and misused I felt. How stupid I was to think he would ever appreciate me. Besides, I had a good-looking, intelligent, stable man beside me who cared and loved me, and here I was tossing it all away.

I reached up and rubbed the stubble on De'Andre's unshaven face, appreciating how lucky I was to have him in my life. Finally realizing this was the man I was born to be with, to marry, to grow old with. No one else compared to him. No one else, not even fucking Vijay Khakwani. He didn't rule these parks anymore. I was tired of him, and I was sure he was tired of me. De'Andre looked down at me and gave me a you're-all-mine kiss, which I was happy to reciprocate. I heard more bumping and thrashing in the hallway. I wondered if Vijay was trying to get my attention by making all this racket. I was pretty sure he was. He did immature shit like that.

However, I caught myself a couple of times staring at the door, itching to open it to see his beautiful face one last time. I didn't think I could ever be just his friend without that sexual attraction being there. I'd tried and failed. I saw my phone light up on the coffee table. It was Vijay saying, *I'm finished moving everything out. Are you home?* I placed the phone back onto the coffee table without responding and cuddled up tighter against De'Andre's chest. He didn't pay much attention to what had transpired and stayed glued to the TV, perhaps fantasizing about our dream home being as beautifully decorated as the ones on TV.

All of a sudden, we jumped at a loud knock at the door. De'Andre and I looked at each other. I signaled to De'Andre to answer it and mouthed, "I'm not here." De'Andre gave me a baffled look but shrugged his broad shoulders and opened the door. I jogged to the inside bedroom so Vijay wouldn't see me.

CONFUSED SPICE

I heard muffled voices going back and forth at the front door, and the conversation was brief. After De'Andre had closed the door, I sauntered out the bedroom with my arms folded against my chest.

"Who was it?" I asked, knowing damn well who it was.

"It was that dude, Vijay," said De'Andre, still looking confused. I asked him what Jay wanted and he said, "When I opened the door, Vijay was kind of shocked to see me. I think he was expecting you to open the door. But anyway, he said today was his last day living here and he wanted to say goodbye. He gave me a handshake and then a long, lingering hug." We both looked at each other with a bemused expression. I didn't know Vijay liked De'Andre that much. I guess he wasn't averse to him after all.

As I strode back to the couch, I said, "Well, he's gone now. No more loud music when we walk into the hallway. Now we can have peace and quiet." I dusted off the pain I felt in my heart.

"There is one last thing,"

I turned toward him as I plopped onto the couch.

"What?"

"The hug was for you."

26

Vijay

After unpacking some of my clothes and placing them in my old closet, I walked into my grandmother's room at the end of the long hallway. She was reading a children's book to my little sister, who was cuddled up next to her with a relaxed smile. They were startled when they heard my footsteps. "Bacha! Come sit." That was what my sister loved to call me. It means "brother" in Hindi. "Nana was just reading me a story."

"Hey, sis, do you mind if I speak to nana for a bit?" I asked, pinching her nose.

"Sure, if you promise to read it to me later."

"Yo, do I ever let you down?" She bounced off the bed, gave me a sisterly kiss on the cheek, and took off out the room with a salute like her favorite YouTuber, Superwoman, who she'd met

CONFUSED SPICE

personally through Suhana. It turned out Suhana and Lilly Singh had attended York University together and remained friends to this day.

"How are you, darling?"

"Not good."

"Have a seat," said my grandmother. Her bangles rattled as she patted the bed. "What's on your mind?"

"Is it true that you thought I should have an arranged marriage?" Before answering, she fixed the *paloo* on her shoulder and pushed up her glasses against her nose.

"Yes, it's true, dear. It's a part of our culture."

"But we're Guyanese, and my mother didn't have one. Why should I have to go through with it? It doesn't make sense."

"Not true, darling, your mother did have one."

"She did?" I said, shocked.

"Yes, she had an arranged marriage with your father, your real father, darling." She paused and then rose from the bed to her dresser. She came back with an old picture and placed it in my hand. I stared down at the picture. There were two young people in traditional Indian wedding garments. I recognized the young woman as my mother. She wore a rich red and gold sari with painted *henna* on her arms and feet. Her hair was parted down the middle and pulled into a neat bun. I'd never seen her look so beautiful and so traditional. But she wore an icy stare; a stare that I couldn't read. Next to her sat a slender young man with a thick, heavy mustache that set well against his dark skin. He wore a beaded white sherwani and a decorative red turban. He looked like an older version of myself. It dawned on me that this was the first time I ever saw my biological father.

"Why did they separate?" A question I hadn't asked before out of respect for Frank, since he had a hand in raising me.

203

"He was a heavy drinker and abused your mother, dear. It was a good thing we left India."

"India?"

"Yes, India."

I felt my hand crinkling the photo. I couldn't believe this was the kind of blood I had coursing through my veins. Was this what I would become? A drunk, a low-life, a wife-beater? Was this the reason why my mother sought therapy when she came to Canada? Was this the reason why she despised me so much — because I reminded her of him? The man she despised? A past that she tried so desperately to forget? It all started to make sense. The puzzle I'd tried so long to put together.

"Your father became very violent, especially when we didn't give him a dowry," said my grandmother, studying my face. "Do you know what a dowry is son?" I nodded. "Well ...your grandfather had at that time lost his job at a clothing factory and didn't have much of a financial income. This left us in a tight financial situation. We went from living in a comfortable downtown apartment to the slums of Mumbai. We stayed with our maid at the time, sharing a small boxed space where we all slept on the cemented floor." She paused as if reliving the experience and then continued. "And your grandfather thought it would be best for your mother to have an arranged marriage to improve our circumstances. Your grandfather couldn't bear seeing his only daughter living in such squalor. It pained him every night, until one day he found a suitable boy for her through a good friend. Your grandfather died two days after your mother married, due to a heart attack. I used your mother's dowry to pay for his funeral arrangements. This infuriated your father's family, the Khakwanis. They accused me of being a deceitful widower and thought I hid the money. I told your father, Joshi, that we didn't

CONFUSED SPICE

have any money. We were poor. But they went on calling me a liar.

"When your mother and I moved into Joshi's flat in Andheri, that's when the abuse began. Joshi said if I dared to interfere in their marriage, he would give me a good thrashing too, which made me and your mother nervous. She asked me to promise not to ever provoke him to do such a thing, and I told her I wouldn't. Everything she did wasn't good enough in his eyes, nor in his family's.

"He yelled and screamed at your mother when she had a miscarriage. It was a baby girl. The Khakwanis fed nasty rumors into Joshi's mind, saying she wasn't 'fit' to bear him children, let alone a boy. This enraged Joshi, and the beatings became severe.

"A few years later, I held Mina's hand as she cried and pushed out a beautiful baby boy who she named Vijay after her father. Everyone rejoiced. It looked as if it was the proudest moment in Joshi's life as he held his first-born baby boy in his arms. The beatings subsided once again and things started to look better between Joshi and Mina. But the peace between them was short-lived when Joshi lost his job as a taxi driver and was reduced to become a chai-*wallah*. Meanwhile, your mother had grown more discontented in her marriage. She blamed me relentlessly for setting up such a union. I told her, me and her father had no choice, or we would've been living in the streets like pariahs. She had become depressed and cried every night on the apartment's terrace where I would bring her dinner, which she didn't eat. During these crazy fits, Joshi would just stare at her as if she was a disease in his life. He would tell me not to comfort her, because she was an ungrateful *chootia*. And in her defense, I would tell him that my daughter wasn't an idiot. But he would just click his tongue and walk out to get drunk at a local bar. For months,

Mina would lay balled up in bed, leaving me with all the cooking and cleaning. I empathized with my Mina, but I also knew there were other women in tougher marriages. No marriage was perfect, I reminded her. But she would just wave me off and go to her room to sulk.

"One day, I told her that she could not just sit up in the house all day and fade away like an old dish rag. I encouraged her to go out. I made a list of items for her to pick up at the store. She took it and came back in a better mood.

"Over a course of the month, she was in better spirits. She would prepare Joshi's favorite meals like mutton curry and *saag paneer*, spiced just the way he liked it served with fresh *chapatis* and tangy mango chutney. She also gave him oiled shoulder massages after his long days of work and brought him hot ginger tea. She finally was behaving like a respectable Indian wife.

"However, I noticed whenever I sent Mina on an errand, she would come back late. One morning I had the next-door neighbor's maid look after my duties as I followed Mina to the market to see who she was meeting up with. My driver followed the rick in front of him from Andheri to Kandivali. Along the way I covered my mouth with my *paloo* so I wouldn't be recognized. A half hour later we arrived in front of a Café Coffee Day. Before getting out the rick I watched Mina slip her driver a few crumpled rupees and make a beeline for the café and hug a *firingi* who sat near a big window. I had no idea who this foreigner was. I took a rick back to the flat and awaited Mina's return. I was going to give her a good talking to.

"The moment she came in the door. I came out of the kitchen in a huff.

"'Mina, where were you?' I shook my finger.

"'I was at the market, *amma*.'

CONFUSED SPICE

"'Do not lie to me, or you will get two tight slaps. Do you have any idea what time it is? No respectable married woman should be out gallivanting at this hour like some *chokri*. Joshi will be home any minute from work.'

"'I just lost track of time. I will get dinner ready,' she said, brushing pass me into the kitchen while adjusting her *paloo* around her neck.

"'Who was that *firingi* that I saw you with this morning?'

"'Did you follow me?'

"'Mina, if Joshi finds out that you are...'

"'How could you!' she exclaimed.

"'I am looking out for you, dear. Now, I forbid you to see that *firingi* anymore. This is foolish behavior.'

"'No.'

"'Mina! I mean it. I won't stand for it. I do not want my daughter to end up like those stupid women living on the streets because of some silly, fleeting romance. Now start being a good wife, because if you continue seeing that *firingi*, people will start to think something is wrong with your marriage.'

"'Well ... let them talk,' she hissed.

"'Have you gone mad?'

"'*Amma*, I love him,' she confessed, stepping toward me with passionate eyes.

"'Does he know you're married?'

"'I told him, he doesn't care. I told him how unhappy I am in this godforsaken marriage.'

"'I won't hear any more of this.' I waved my hand dismissively.

"Right before I entered my room, she said, 'I'm pregnant.'

"Silence filled the room. I turned halfway around and looked at her. She looked at me with fright in her eyes. I looked down and saw she had a hand resting on her flat stomach.

"'What have you done?'

"'I'm leaving this hell hole, that's what I'm doing.'

"'And where exactly will you go?'

"'I'm going to Canada with Frank. We're going to get married.'

"'I forbid it, Mina. If your father were here to hear such words coming from your insolent mouth.'

"'He would approve.'

"A few minutes later, Joshi walked in from work and the conversation ceased. Mina prepared dinner while I went to my room and sat on the edge of the bed, wondering what would happen to us once Joshi found out this news. I pulled out the Holy Quran from the side table drawer and said a fervent prayer.

"A few weeks had passed, and Mina continued to see this foreigner after Joshi left for work. As far as I could tell, he didn't think anything was out of the ordinary, which had been a blessing in disguise. I watched as Mina brushed and pressed her long black hair, like she did for school. She then rummaged through the closet for the best-looking *kameeze* while I stood in the doorway with my arms folded against my chest in disapproval, but she paid me little mind. As she butterflied around the room, there was a deafening knock at the door. Mina and I looked at each other in horror. I answered it, but it was only the milk boy. After I closed the door I went back to the room to talk sense into Mina.

"'This has gone on long enough.'

"'We've been through this, and I'm seeing him.'

"'How could you disobey your mother; do you have any shame?'

"'*Ammaji*, I'm leaving.'

"I stood guard at the bedroom door, blocking her path and shaking a finger at her as if she was a naughty child. 'This is foolish. What are you trying to do, na? What if your husband finds out and throws us both out onto the streets? Stop and think, you stupid child. Think about your mother. Think about Vijay. Think about your family name.'

"'Move,' was her only response.

"'No.'

"'Move, you old woman!' she shouted. I slapped her face and shook her senseless, damning her actions. She wiggled out of my grasp and held her injured cheek with both hands.

"'I don't want to live this life. Why can't you understand that? I'm not you, nor the other common women in India. I want much more for myself,' she shouted.

"'Oh yeah? Doing what? Being an adulterer?'

"'Why can't I be happy?'

"'You silly girl, do you know how lucky you have it? Now stop behaving like a greedy woman and attend to your duties as a good wife. I am done talking about this. I'm not going to let you bring any more shame to this family. You're going to get rid of that baby, and you're not going to see that guy anymore.'

"'I'm not, and I'm going to see him. I can go during your naps. There's nothing you can do to stop me.'

"I grabbed her by the arm, and she snatched it away. 'Stop this now.'

"'No, I'm leaving, *ammaji*.' She brushed past me and placed her hand on the doorknob.

"'Don't you walk out that door!' I demanded. Then there was a click.

"One scorching hot afternoon, as I was sitting on the couch watching my soaps, Mina walked through the door with two tourist visas, waving them in my face.

"'How did you get those?'

209

MATHIS BAILEY

"'Don't worry about it, this is our ticket out of here.'

"'Mina, you cannot go through with this, na,' I said, following her into the kitchen to get dinner ready.

"'How come, *ammaji*? It's miserable here. You see how Joshi and his family treat us. It's unbearable. We're no better off than maids.'

"'This *firingi* ... is he Muslim?'

"'He's agnostic.'

"'Agnostic? You must convert him to Islam.'

"'Why does it matter?'

"'It matters a great deal.'

"'Okay, we will do it once we are in Canada.'

"'Canada?'

"'Yes, Canada. I'm pretty sure he won't mind converting. He loves me. You hear me mom, he loves me. He truly does.' She stared warmly into my eyes. I looked at her for a moment and then down at the visas in her hand.

"The next morning, Mina had served Joshi his usual breakfast: chai tea, *roti* with scrambled eggs. She behaved like any other day, not letting on to her plan. After he left for work, she gathered all our things and threw them into two big suitcases. She spun around on her heels and grabbed everything that she needed to make our journey as comfortable as possible. I stood by, watching her in fright with a hand over my mouth. This was total madness. There was a knock at the front door. Mina froze and looked up at me in horror then stared at the filled suitcases lying on the bed. I wiped the sweat from my forehead with the edge of my *paloo* before answering it. I opened the door and it was Joshi's mother, Indira. She had come over to watch her soaps. She didn't like watching her soaps alone ... so me and Mina would watch

210

CONFUSED SPICE

them with her while she ate rice and *daal* and clicked her tongue at the TV whenever something scandalous happened.

"As Indira sat on the sofa, she grabbed a Bollywood magazine from the coffee table and fanned herself with it.

"'Why this flat so hot? Open up the windows,' Indira said viciously. Mina slid the living room windows open. The caws of the crows could be heard from a neighboring tree. Indira looked suspiciously at me and Mina.

"'How come this house still looks the way it does? Did Mina do any cleaning at all today?' she asked, clicking her tongue against her one tooth as she picked up a dirty plate from the coffee table that Joshi had left behind this morning and handed it to Mina.

"'Mina isn't feeling all that well,' I said.

"After placing the dirty plate in the sink, Mina started to sweep the marble white floors with a bundle of thin, wispy sticks while holding up one end of her sari.

"'Do not forget to do over here,' said Indira. 'It's a mess.'

"'Would you like some tea? I was just about to put some on,' I asked.

"'*Nae nae,* I just had some on my way here. My maid makes the best chai tea. I don't like the way it tastes over here. I think it's the water,' she said with a dismissive wave. 'Where's my son, Joshi? I was hoping I catch him before he left for work. I need to tell him something that I heard on the streets.' Mina looked alarmed. Indira continued. 'Apparently, he got some Brahmin woman sick at his chai stall. She is discouraging people to drink his tea.' I heard Mina let out a sigh of relief. 'I'll tell you, these middle-class Indians are not strong enough to survive here anymore. They just as bad as these foreigners.' she said, clicking her tongue.

MATHIS BAILEY

"Two hours later, when Joshi's mother went back home, Mina and I resumed our packing. We went down to the apartment lobby and flagged a rickshaw. We met the foreigner at Café Mondegar. The foreigner had a gentle expression. He wore faded jeans and a white kurta and was carrying a brown leather backpack. His hair was short and golden blonde. He looked like the white men in those American movies.

"'You must be Mina's mother. Nice to meet you,' he said, bowing his head. I looked at him warily and wobbled my head in response, too frightened to say a word. I pulled my *paloo* over my head so I wouldn't be recognized and suggested Mina do the same, which she did not hesitate to do. She wanted everything to go perfectly.

"We took the elevator to a hotel above the cafe. The room was spacious with potted plants scattered throughout.

"'Would anyone like me to order room service?' asked Frank.

"'Yes, Mom and I will have a cup of tea,' said Mina, sitting on the bed and massaging the sole of her foot. I heard Frank place in an order for two teas and one coffee. When the drinks arrived, Mina and Frank sat on the sofa and discussed the plane arrangements. We would arrive in Toronto tomorrow morning. He dug into his brown bag and unearthed four plane tickets. Mina came over to the window where I was sitting and showed me the tickets. I asked her how she had gotten everything done so quickly. She responded that Frank was a social worker in Canada and that he had managed to pull some strings at the Canadian Embassy.

"Soon, we were at Mumbai airport and boarded our flight. I sat back in my seat, looking out the window at the black tarmac. It dawned on me that I had never been outside of Mumbai, let alone India. I looked over to Mina, who looked relieved and liberated. I touched her hand and she touched mine as the plane took off, taking us to a strange land."

27

Pierre

few days had gone by since Vijay moved out.
I couldn't believe how much I missed him. I couldn't
believe how much I would miss the blaring music coming from his apartment. Now, when I came home from work, I
heard nothing. Vijay was no longer here, no longer asking me
to come over to cook. No more sharing intimate stories about
our past. No more confiding into each other when we needed
someone the most. One day, as I was coming home from work,
I pressed my ear against Vijay's door. Silence. I tried to imagine
the place bare without the dilapidated sofa. The sofa on which
we'd shared so many moments. I tried to imagine the sweet scent
of his place. How wonderful it smelled of orange blooms and pas-
sionfruit with a light scent of the fabric softener he used. Now,
I realized my oasis was gone. I felt saddened and abandoned. I

wanted him back. This could not be happening to me, to us. It wasn't supposed to turn out this way. I pressed my hand on the door, trying to provoke memories. One came to mind when we were cooking. He blew turmeric in my face, and I was a yellow mess, then I threw paprika at him and he looked like Satan. Within a few seconds, it was Holi in his kitchen. Our own little festival. It took us hours to clean up, but we had fun doing it, laughing mostly the whole time at our shenanigans.

After freshening up, Jay offered me his clothes that he had pulled from his closet. I slipped on his black T-shirt and baggy Nike track pants. After I got dressed, I still smelled like turmeric. I asked if he had some cologne. "You know what! I have a better idea. Why don't we swap colognes?" I asked him why, and he said, "Because I love the way you smell yo."

Oh my god ... he loves the way I smell. It was rare that he paid me compliments that weren't related to my cooking. But I found it odd that he wanted to smell like me. But I went across the hall and grabbed my favorite cologne, Paco Rabanne: 1 Million.

We traded, and he sprayed it at the base of his neck. "Now I smell like a million bucks." He smiled. He handed me a black bottle with a blue star on it. The smell was strong and spicy. Not something I would normally wear, but it smelled like Vijay. I thought this would be the closest I would ever get to him.

I snapped out my reverie, took my ear away from his door, and went over to my apartment. I walked in and looked around for De'Andre. He was out. I tossed the keys on the kitchen counter and poured myself a glass of wine. My mind drifted back to Vijay's apartment. I wondered if he thought of me when he wore my cologne that day. I wondered if he played with himself as my signature scent tangled up his beautifully sculpted nose. The thought aroused me. I took my glass off the counter and went

CONFUSED SPICE

over to the sofa. I thought about blogging about a new French restaurant that Dre had taken me to a few days ago on Wellington Street called Colette Grand Café. The tuna tartare was delicious, and the eggs Benedict melted in my mouth. So creamy. My thoughts came rushing furiously as my laptop powered up. This was definitely the best time to write.

Before I went onto my blog, I checked Facebook. I needed to see Jay's face. I needed to know what he was up to. I searched for his page, but it was no longer available. He must be taking this monk's life really seriously, I thought. I logged off Facebook, went to my food blog, and started typing. After I posted the last food pic, I strolled into the bedroom and sat on the edge of the bed, still nursing my glass of wine. I took a sip and savored the intense dark cherry flavor, and then tossed back the last drop. I set the empty glass on the night stand and fell back onto the king-size bed, pulled the duvet up to my chin, and fell into a cloud of deep sleep.

28

Vijay

It was midnight. I lay across my bed, thinking about what my grandmother had told me about my mother's past. I couldn't believe my whole life was nothing but a lie. To stop thinking about this shit, I got up and finished unpacking the rest of my clothes from the boxes. I had no choice but to move back home. This was some bullshit. I needed to do something to change the course of my life. My mind suddenly drifted to Pierre. I missed him. I never thought I would develop those kinds of feelings toward another dude. But I had. Strong emotions that I could not fight. I wondered what he was doing at this moment. Was he cooking? Or was he alone? Or was he with that douchebag of a fiancé of his?

After finishing putting away my clothes, I lay back across my bed and reflected again on the story my grandmother had shared

CONFUSED SPICE

with me. All this time I thought I was Guyanese, but I was actually Indian. INDIAN! My parents had lied to me so I wouldn't go searching for my real father. I knew something was up when I asked her about my birth certificate several weeks ago. She was behaving so defensive, asking why I needed it. I told her to see the holy temples that my spiritual friends recommended I see in India. She said it was a foolish idea to go over there with all its corruption and that I needed to focus more on important things like going back to school to get my degree. But I refused to give up so easily. I tossed a shirt back into the box and decided to go to her office. She was sitting behind her desk reading some documents.

"So, are you going to give me my birth certificate?" I said. She looked up from the document she was reading, took off her glasses, and placed them in her hair.

"We've been through this, Vijay," she said in an exasperated tone.

"Stop behaving like a lunatic and give me my birth certificate," I demanded.

"No."

"Why not? What are you hiding?"

"Vijay, get out of my office, I have work to finish," she said, placing on her glasses.

"What you afraid of? That I will find out who my biological parents are?" I can't lie; the possibility often crossed my mind. We barely shared a resemblance. She was fair-skinned, and I'm dark. I remember people used to mistake my mother for my nanny when I was growing up.

"Vijay!"

"Look at me? I'm dark, you're fair," I said.

"Vijay, you are my biological son, so stop with this talk."

217

MATHIS BAILEY

"Mother, do you remember when we went to that pool party at your coworker's house in Mississauga, and all the kids there were white ... and I was the only dark-skinned kid there? They were all staring at me like I was from another planet. Do you have any idea how that made me feel?"

"Vijay, they were staring at me wearing a sari."

"Ha! I think not."

"Vijay, you're my child. End of story."

"Well ... since you won't give it to me, you leave me with no choice." She looked up at me from her stacks of papers and stood up.

"What do you mean, Vijay?"

"I will just have to call the hospital. I'm pretty sure they will have a copy of the record." I knew this wouldn't fly, because I had no clue where I was born.

"Well ... go ahead, Vijay," she said, placing her glasses back on.

"Why are you behaving this way? I am tired of you dictating and deciding how I should live my life."

"I will stop dictating your life when you stop using my money for your silly gallivanting adventures," she said sharply.

"This is bullshit," I said.

"Well ... Vijay, life isn't fair. You will soon learn that."

"Give me the fuckin' document."

"No. You know what, on second thought, perhaps I should let you witness those filthy beggars that lives on the streets in India and let them take advantage of your stupidity and let your fate fall into their hands. Is that what you wish to become, a beggar? Huh? Do you?

"No, I don't but..."

"Good, so stop with this nonsense about going to India to become a monk," she said, waving her hand dismissively.

218

"Just to let you know, the arranged marriage is off."

She was going to say something, but before she could, I was out the door. There was nothing she could do to hold me back from going to India to look for my biological father and becoming a monk. However, there was a possibility she could throw me out of her house again if I didn't comply with this arranged marriage biz. Oh well ... fuck it.

⌒ ⌒

The following morning, I learned from my grandmother the details of where I was birthed. It was Jaslok Hospital in Mumbai. I called it and requested my birth certificate. They faxed it over. Once I had all my credentials in order to get a passport, I logged onto the family's computer in the study room that Frank used as his personal library. I went to the Government of Canada website and downloaded passport documents. As I was filling out the documents, I noticed I needed three non-related people to sign off as references to confirm that I am who I say I am. I knew my parents wouldn't help to get one of their friends to sign. I guess I could ask Navaan, my neighbor, and my boy I worked with at Foot Locker. I thought hard for the last person, and Pierre came in mind.

It started to snow lightly the next morning as I stood on the backyard patio contemplating my next move. I had my hands punched down in my hoodie to keep them warm. I knew I needed to get out of this house, fast. If I stayed here any longer, I would lose my mind. I couldn't stand it anymore. As I leaned against the wooden railing, I took in the crisp air and let the bitter cold breeze brush against my face. Strangely, it felt good. I took another deep breath, and mounds of cold steam escaped from my lips. I placed my hoodie over my head and folded my arms against my chest, staring out into dark cluster of trees. I heard footsteps come up behind me, and I turned around.

"You're, up early, son. Is everything alright?"

"I'm fine, Frank," I said softly. Knowing what he had done for my mother and for us to live a better life made me appreciate him even more. "Thanks for asking."

"Well, I was going to make some breakfast for myself. Would you like some?"

"No, I'm okay. Thanks for asking," I said, turning back around.

A moment of silent passed between us, then Frank spoke. "Vijay, I know I haven't been much of a father to you over the years but…"

"No, you've been a great father, Frank," I said, turning around and cutting him off. I took a few steps toward him. We stared at each other for a bit. I don't think he knew that I knew. I thought about bringing it up but changed my mind.

"I don't know; I feel I could have done better," he said, staring at me.

"You did all you could, Frank," I said.

"Well … don't stress out too much, son. Just try to stay off your mother's bad side. She really means well. She just wants the best for you. That's all."

"I know," I said mildly, almost to myself.

"Try not to stay out here too long, or you will catch a cold. A hoodie and basketball shorts aren't particularly winter attire," he said with a smile.

"I'll be in the house in a few. It was stuffy inside."

"Oh, that's your mother's fault. She prefers the house to be toasty. You will understand once you get to our age." He

CONFUSED SPICE

chuckled. "I will turn down the heat, she's up anyway." He went back inside, pulling the glass patio doors shut.

I heard my mother's voice waking up my sister for school. A few minutes later I walked back into the house and headed toward my room. I thought right now wasn't the time to have the conversation with my mother about my biological father. As I lay across my bed, my mind floated off to Pierre. I had to give him a call to come over and sign these documents. But he hadn't been returning my texts or my calls since I left my old apartment. Perhaps he was still upset with me for behaving like a jerk. I wanted to give him a hug, but my ego prevented me from doing so.

I toyed with my phone and thought about sending him a text. I couldn't do it. I rose out of bed and did some sit-ups and then pushups to relieve some stress. I picked up the phone again. My heart was pumping rapidly as I scrolled through a list of names to find Pierre's. I found his number and sent him a text. From the nightstand I picked up a spiritual book and read a few verses from it: "*In the gap between two thoughts, thought-free wakefulness manifests unceasingly.*" I pondered this over and over.

⸻

Later in the evening, everyone was gone out the house besides my mother and me. Frank had taken my little sister ice skating at Nathan Phillips Square. My grandmother didn't ice skate but Vanessa begged her to come along. Frank asked me if I wanted to go, but told him I was feeling a little under the weather, which wasn't true. But he bought it. Probably because of what I wore this morning on the patio. I just wanted to stay behind to have some alone time with my mother, who was swamped with work and told everyone to go on without her and have fun.

I was thinking about how to start the conversation. I wanted to talk about what I had learned about her past. The past she tried so hard to forget, like the old saris she had shoved away in suitcases at the back of her closet. I wondered what her reaction would be once she knew that I had discovered her truth.

Before I entered her office, my phone vibrated in my pants pocket. It was Pierre. He'd responded to the text I sent this morning. Seeing his name flash across my screen made me smile. I read his text: *Sure, I will be there.* That's my boy. I couldn't wait to see him. Reading his text placed me in a better mood. However, I wasn't looking forward to what I had to do next.

I walked into my mother's office, where she was on a conference call. She stood at the bookcase that held all her law books. She was dressed in her favorite silk white blouse that Frank had bought her for her fiftieth birthday. She wore it with a pearl necklace. I could tell she just got her hair washed and trimmed. I took a seat in the big brown leather chair in the corner and waited. After she hung up from her call she spoke.

"What can I do for you, Vijay?" she said, walking back to her desk, taking a seat and flipping through some paperwork.

"I need you to look at some documents," I said.

"I hope it's not another apartment release form," she said, looking up at me over the rim of her reading glasses.

"No, it's not a release form," I said.

"Good. What is it?"

I looked down at the document in my hands, debating whether or not I should give it to her. Within seconds I would see her perfect world come crashing down. I didn't know if I would be able to handle it myself. I usually sought opportunities like this to take revenge on her kicking me out of her perfect home years ago and for trying to dictate my life, but somehow this situation

CONFUSED SPICE

was different. I knew I was entering dangerous territory, revealing something that was bigger than myself. I rose and tossed a file folder onto her desk. She opened it and examined the sheet of paper inside with slitted eyes. I watched her face morph into different shades of emotion. I sank back in my seat, waiting for a response. Then, all of a sudden she looked up at me in disbelief with a hand covering her agape mouth.

"Who gave you this?" she demanded.

"That's not important," I said.

"Who gave you this!" she exclaimed, rising out her swivel chair and pounding a fist on her oak cherry desk.

"Calm down, yo. I ordered it." She looked down at the paper once again as if she still couldn't believe what was lying before her.

"Why didn't you tell me you were born in India?" I asked.

"Vijay, did your grandmother tell you?"

I kept quiet, allowing the deep silence answer for me.

"Vijay, there's something I need to tell you," she said, sighing and sitting back in her chair, slowly trying to collect herself. I'd never seen her look this way before, so vulnerable, so hopeless. She took a breath, stared at me for a moment, and spoke. "I moved to Canada so I could have a better life, so *you* could have a better life. So you can have all the opportunities before you." She took another deep breath. "I swore to myself that I wouldn't be a housewife like the women in my family. I wanted to have a choice to choose who I wanted to be in life and who I wanted to love. However, I was robbed of that. Stuck in someone else's life that was not my own." She rose and strolled to the long window while clutching her necklace as if in a distant memory. "Vijay, I didn't want you to grow up seeing me like that, a housewife, not valued no more than a pariah on the street. If I would've stayed

223

MATHIS BAILEY

with your father, it would have been hell for me ... and for you."
She turned around and stared at me with her black mascara running down her pale face. "Vijay, I don't want you to go to India to look him up. I don't want him to come looking for us. There's no telling what he may do. That's why I hadn't told you. That is why I told you we were from Guyana. I know it was wrong, but I had to do it for the safety of our family."

"Mother, I know you did what you had to do, and have no quarrel with that. But I'm a grown man. If I want to see my father, I should have the right to do so," I said resolutely. It wasn't my intention to see my real father, but since she brought it up, I wouldn't mind seeing the man that brought me into this world. Besides, he had probably changed.

"Vijay, I forbid you to go."

"I'm going whether you like it or not."

She wiped the tears away with a Kleenex and came around her desk and leaned against it. "Vijay, what do you want? Is it money? Do you want me to write you a check so you can find a place in Toronto? Perhaps somewhere in the heart of downtown?"

"Mother! Enough with your bribery. You can't blind me with shiny things anymore. I know the truth, and I accepted it," I said.

"Vijay, I forbid you to go to India, and that's that," she said, taking a seat and placing on her glasses.

"I knew it would come down to this," I said, snatching the paper off her desk.

"Vijay, stop!" she said, rising from her chair. "What is this really about?"

I turned around slowly, thinking about what she meant.

"You know what this is about? I want to visit India to be a..."

"This is about that boy, Pierre, isn't it?"

CONFUSED SPICE

"Are you saying I like dudes?" I said, shocked that my own mother was calling me out.

"Vijay, I've been watching you, and I know you're going down the wrong path."

"Man, whatever," I said, turning to leave.

"Vijay!"

"Yes," I said, stopping in my tracks with my back to her.

"Don't make any mistakes that you may regret."

With that I left her office.

29

Pierre

It was 10:45 at night, and my phone vibrated on the coffee table. The text said, *I need to see you. Please come now.*

My heart pounded inside my chest. What should I do? I looked at De'Andre, who was sitting next to me on the sofa, staring at my phone and waiting for me to tell him who it was, as if he was gatekeeper of my incoming calls. When I didn't say anything, he said, "Who was that?"

"Vijay," I plainly said.

"What does he want?" he said, irritably rubbing a hand over his chiseled face.

"I don't know exactly, but he needs to see me. It sounds urgent."

"You're not his psychiatrist; you can't go running every time he's in trouble."

CONFUSED SPICE

"You don't understand."

"Oh really, help me understand." He sat up straighter on the sofa with his chest puffed out looking Romanesque.

"Don't make this a big deal, Andre," I said, slipping into my red Converse and reaching for the car keys. By the time I grabbed them, we were face to face, standing near the door. I placed a hand on his smooth chest, feeling the pulsation of his rapid heartbeat. "I will be back shortly," I cooed. He gave me a wary expression, but the lines on his forehead relaxed. I gave him a weak smile and walked out the door.

Jay's street was well lit with European-style black street lamps. Neighborhood watch signs were practically on every corner. I couldn't remember where the house was, so I drove in circles. "Driving while black" paranoia had started to kick in. I prayed I wouldn't get pulled over by the police or some overzealous neighborhood watch guard due to some call-in by a xenophobic prick suspecting suspicious behavior. I kept driving, cautious of my surroundings. Every house looked identical, with the same peachy brick and white door. I took out the piece of paper that I'd written the address on and consulted it. I peered through the night trying to read addresses on houses. As I drove, I saw a dark figure wearing a hoodie standing in the street. When I got closer, I saw it was Vijay. I stopped, and he jumped in as if he had just robbed a bank.

"What are you doing out here?" I said. "I almost ran you over."

"I saw you drive by a couple times and decided to come out. I figured you were lost."

"Oh."

"Why didn't you just call, yo?"

"I left my cell at home."

MATHIS BAILEY

He looked at me for a moment and then looked around in the car. "This is a nice ride. I've never been in a Maserati before." He pressed the power button above him that opened the sunroof. It slid back with a smooth, metallic sound; then he pressed the button that adjusted his seat. He reclined back with his long legs suggestively open with his basketball shorts hiked up, exposing inches of his thighs.

"Why did you need to see me tonight?" I asked. He took out a folded paper and handed it to me. "What is this?"

"It's my passport papers."

"For what?"

"To travel," he said plainly.

"I know, but why are you showing me this, and where are you going?"

"I want to go to India, but to get my passport I need a third signature on these forms."

I perused the forms and saw two signature boxes signed.

"Why can't one of your parents' friends sign this?"

"Because my mother doesn't want me to go."

"Why?" He shrugged and gazed out the window.

"Does it have anything to do with your engagement?"

"What?" he said, sitting up. "Who told you that?"

"So, it's true?"

"Well yeah, but I called it off."

"How come?"

"It was some stupid arranged marriage that my mother wanted me to have. The whole thing was not me yo."

"But I thought you were Guyanese."

"Dude, it's a long story."

"Okay."

228

CONFUSED SPICE

"So how did you find out about the arranged marriage?" he asked.

"Your mother."

"My mother?"

"Yeah, she called and told me about the engagement," I said. I thought it was best not to tell him about the threat she'd made. I didn't need any more drama in my life.

"Well ... it's not happening."

"Jay"

"Yes?"

"How did your mother get my number?" I asked.

"Probably when she was doing wedding invitations. She asked me for a list of contacts of the people I wanted to invite. Your name and information was on the list."

I said "Oh," and looked out the window and then back at Jay. "So, what is the reason for this trip to India?"

"Don't laugh yo but..." He paused to study my expression. "I want to become a monk."

My eyebrows shot up. "Are you sure, Vijay? Do you know what becoming a monk means?"

"Yeah, I'm already practicing abstinence and abstaining from liquor."

"And how long have you been practicing?" This was for my own information. I wanted to know if he'd been with anyone sexually since we met.

"Almost five months."

Around the time we met. I wondered if I had anything to do with him becoming a monk. No, impossible. He couldn't be becoming a monk to escape from choosing a sexual preference.

MATHIS BAILEY

"Also, Vijay, just to let you know, abstaining from sex also means not masturbating. How have you been handling that?" I saw his Adam's apple take a dip.

"Now, that's been pretty hard. But I'm working on it. I haven't touched myself since..." He paused. "For a couple months."

I felt my body getting warmer. He hadn't touched himself in months. My sexual senses were telling me he was horny. I wondered if this was the main reason why he'd asked me to come over this late, and not just to sign this document. I mean, why couldn't it wait till morning? He'd brought me out here to sex me up. I felt my manhood harden with the thought. I wondered if he wanted to do it here in the car. *Is he that freaky?* I look at the clock on the dashboard; it was well after midnight. I'd told Dre I would be back shortly. Two hours flew by with a blink of an eye. Time seemed to collapse whenever I was with Vijay. To fight the bulge in my pants, I looked down at the document to take my mind off it.

"So..." he said.

"I'll sign it."

Hearing this made him smile from ear to ear like those black cats that smile on the ticking clocks. I rummaged through the glove department for a pen.

"There!" I said, handing it to him with a smile.

"You're my boy, Pierre. Thank you."

"You're welcome, but I think I should be going, Jay."

"But I have to repay you, man. Is there anything open? Are you hungry?"

"It's almost one o'clock, I don't think so. Besides, I'm not hungry. I had dinner before I came."

He looked as if he didn't want the night to end. But he knew there was nothing he could do to make me stay. We weren't at his apartment anymore. He couldn't pull out any magic tricks.

There was a delicious silence between us.

"Let me see your hand," I said rather boldly. I decided to use my own magic tricks. He gave me his hand with much alacrity. "You have nice hands."

"Really?" he said, flipping the one in my hands as if trying to find the beauty in it.

I started to massage it, and his hand became lifeless in mine. He laid back in his seat and closed his eyes. I felt my sex getting up again and I wondered if his was too. I kept pressing the key points in his hand: the fleshy parts, then between the fingers. His hand felt so warm and clammy. His nails were clean and nicely cut at the base. I studied the crevices and deep lines coursing down his palms. He moaned as I hit the tender spots. I pressed harder and soft moans escaped from his beautiful lips. His long legs spread wider. Should I dare? My inner voice told me not to cross the line. But I wanted to. I worked my way from his hand to his arm and found my way to his thigh. I pressed and worked up slowly. There was no confused space; just us taunting the air with sex. When I was about to go further up, he stopped me.

"No."

I withdrew my hand from his shorts. "What?"

"We can't do this."

"Why?" I knew the answer already, but I didn't want to stop now. Vijay looked out the window. I followed his gaze and saw nothing but a jungle of trees wrapped up in the night. "What are you looking at?"

"Pierre," he said, still looking ahead, "just imagine a dark figure coming along down that walkaway, planning on ruining your life. Do you stay on that path with the dark figure or cross the street?" I didn't say anything. I looked at the night and then back at Vijay. I knew what he meant, but I wasn't sure which of us was that dark figure. I backed away and fell back on the car window. There was a long silence.

"Vijay, I think I should go, it's late." Vijay gave me a long stare which I broke away.

"Goodnight, Pierre," he said before shutting the door to the car.

I felt this was the last time we would see each other, and he felt it too. But we both knew it was for the best.

As I drove home, I pondered what Vijay actually meant about the dark figure on the sidewalk. But whatever it meant, I felt my relationship with Vijay had officially come to an end. However, tonight I sensed he had been thinking about me the way I'd been thinking about him. Not in so many words but with his actions. The way he was staring into my eyes tonight, I could sense he wanted to press his lips against mine in such a way that would let the world know about us, and I wouldn't have stopped him. But I knew he respected my relationship with Dre.

In a few weeks Vijay would be in India, where there was chaotic traffic and exotic spices perfuming the air. He would be exploring and becoming wiser. I was happy for him, yet there were times I felt bankrupt of his love; a love that would be thousands of miles around the world; a love that would be not feasible. Not tangible. Not attainable. If only he didn't have to travel halfway around the world to feel loved and accepted. But that was the price he was willing to pay to find peace, which we are all looking for, the fabric of our true selves.

CONFUSED SPICE

The following morning, I heard De'Andre draw the living room curtain and start the shower. I climbed out of bed, sauntered into the kitchen, and started the coffee maker. After he finished showering and throwing on his clothes, I handed him a cup of coffee. He didn't mention anything about me coming home late last night from Jay's place. When I got back that night, he was out like a lamp. I noticed he'd polished off a bottle of Merlot, which sat on the living room coffee table. He must've been upset with me, but if he was he didn't show it now as he watched TV. It looked as if something else was bothering him. I guessed he was stressed out from work and writing the manuscript for his book.

Later in the evening, De'Andre left to have a couple of drinks with his colleagues at the Bier Markt downtown. I sat at home wanting to talk to someone about my life. I had no idea where it was headed. I felt Dre and I were drifting apart again. I didn't know how to fix it. I thought about calling my mother. She'd dealt with heartache before when my father cheated on her. And I could talk to her about my relationship with Dre. She was more accepting to our relationship. My father was still a work in progress. Whenever we talked, he didn't inquire about my relationship with Dre. But when Dre and I went home for the holidays to visit, my father would pat Dre on the back and share laughs with him about guy things. But my dad was getting there. My mom was the first one I'd told about Dre and me. I remember her sitting at the dining room table cutting out Kroger coupons from a shopping pamphlet. I came to her and told her I had something important to tell her. She detected the earnestness of the matter and slowly lowered the scissors onto the long, polished mahogany table.

MATHIS BAILEY

She asked if everything was okay, and I said yes. I told her about me being in love with Dre, with no fluff, and that I was gay. I'd been spending a lot of time with Dre, who I'd been referring to as my roommate. My mother's face was stoic and then gradually took on a confused look. She asked if I had problems getting a girlfriend. This made me chuckle a bit. I had no problem getting girls. There wasn't a day that went by that I wasn't hit on. However, I didn't have sex with them. I liked men. I told her that Dre was the one, and she stared at the scattered multi-colored coupons and then back at me and said I would always be her son and there was nothing that would change that. I gave her a hug and felt a huge weight lifted from my chest.

I dialed her number, and it rang for a few seconds before she picked up.

"Hey, baby."

"Hi, Mom."

"I haven't heard from you in a while. Have you spoken to your brother and sister?"

"Not really. I have been really busy." The truth of matter was I had my own shit to deal with rather than hearing somebody else's.

"I understand, dear, but be sure to give your sister a call."

I rolled my eyes and let out a light sigh. "I will when I get a chance."

"Be sure you do, because I spoke to your sister and she is going through things."

"Like what?"

"Like losing her job and dealing with these no-good guy friends of hers."

"It's because she picks them up on the street or at the club."

"Talk to her, she will listen to her little brother. I did all I could do. Talking to that girl makes my head turn to mush."

"If you can't get through to her, I know I won't be of any use, either."

"Well, it doesn't hurt to try, baby."

"Okay, Mom. I will."

"So, son, what's been going on with you? Have you and Dre set a wedding date yet?"

"Not yet, but I was thinking about May."

"Spring is a wonderful time to get married. I can't wait to come up there to see my sons."

"I can't wait to see you too."

"How's Dre?"

"He's okay."

I was feeling more and more reluctant to tell my mother about what was going on in my life. She had grown so fond of De'Andre. Every time Dre and I went back to Detroit, he would spoil my mother rotten with expensive gifts and boxes of Godiva chocolates and entertain her with colorful stories about me sleeping in all day. And she would laugh and say, "Yeah, that sounds like Pierre."

"Mom..."

"Yes, dear."

"I am having second thoughts about getting married."

"Why, honey? Having cold feet is normal."

"It's not cold feet. I just don't think I'm ready," I managed to say without painting Dre as the bad guy.

"Well, baby, just listen to the Holy Spirit. It will guide you to the right place. And you will thank it. So don't you worry too much. Worrying doesn't do any good for the soul."

"I'll make sure I won't."

"You sound so down, baby, are you sure everything is alright?"

I took a breath. "De'Andre cheated on me," I choked out. The phone went silent for a moment.

"Are you okay?"

"No, I feel I'm not enough for him anymore. I mean, he apologized and everything, but I have my doubts about the whole matter. I just don't want to get caught up in anything that I will have to regret later."

"I understand, baby. I know this is a very hard time for you and De'Andre, but you two must pull through it. You know, when your father cheated on me I was devastated. I thought I was going to lose my mind. I found out by going through his wallet and finding a picture of him with some children that I had never seen before, and one of them looked just like you. I remember confronting your father about it, holding up the picture. He denied the affair. But later the guilt got to him and he told me the truth. I felt so betrayed. Not only by him, but by his family who knew about it. I slept in the guest room for days on end, not knowing what to do, so I turned to the Lord for help."

"Then what?" I asked.

"I heard the Holy Spirit ask me, 'Where does your anchor hold?' And I knew where it was held: in God's hands. I had placed my marriage into God's hands." She took a breath and went on. "Our marriage was fine after that, but baby, do what works for you."

After I hung up, I sat there thinking about my relationship with De'Andre. I couldn't go on like this wondering if I was enough for him or wondering if he was out sleeping with someone else. I was pretty sure my mother thought the same thing in her marriage during those sleepless nights when she paced the floors waiting for the man she loved to come home. Even though my parents were still married, they didn't live together anymore. When my father had a stroke a few years ago, she found it difficult to take care of him. The family agreed to set him up in an assistant living home. She visited him every week: cooking, cleaning and doing his laundry. She was almost like his personal maid. However, I could tell my mom enjoyed the independence. She told me whenever she went to visit my father he would apologize for the affair, and how much he loved her. She would ask him why it happened? He would just shrug. She forgave him nonetheless, and would leave with a soft kiss on his forehead.

30

Pierre

I felt De'Andre get out of bed and stroll into the kitchen. I got up, went to the bathroom and splashed water on my face, and stared into the mirror. I couldn't believe I was about to do this. After what I learned this morning, I had to. I walked back out into the living room. De'Andre was on the sofa eating take-out food that I'd brought home today from work. I sat next to him and asked if he loved me. He said yes. I asked him to ask me the same, and he was shocked to find the response different. He rose and strode to the window with his muscular back flexed. He told me I was making a big mistake and that I didn't mean it, but he knew deep down I did. He had broken his trust as a lover. I refused to be like my mother, in a trapped marriage just to be financially secure. I would not live that life. I decided to take another path. That was one of the reasons why I didn't want to date Dre in the first place, because I didn't like the fact that he had more than me. He'd finished college, landed a prestigious job, and had it all figured out, whereas I was the opposite. I used to say to myself, *I will never end up in my mother's predicament.* And look at me now; I was her. It's funny how life plays out. It's funny that we say we will never be like our parents, but at the end we are just like them. This was a challenging time for me to decide my future and I had.

Instead of arguing like we usually did, I rose silently, went into the bedroom, and packed my things.

"Where will you stay?" he asked, following me inside the room. I didn't know. I thought about my options. I thought about Octavia and remembered she was in British Columbia visiting family. She was the only close friend I had in Canada. Everyone else was just acquaintances. I had no place to go. I kept this thought to myself and kept packing. Dre stared at me, dumbstruck, as if he couldn't believe I was actually serious. He tried to block me from leaving, but I brushed passed him with bags in hand.

When I went to the door, he tried stopping me once again. The look in his hazel eyes was not of anger but of sorrow. A tear dropped from one, and I wiped it with my hand. I didn't know what to do to ease his pain for the both of us, but I knew if I stayed it would be out of manipulation. I couldn't allow us to continue down this road. It had gone on for far too long. Pretend time was over. This show had come to an end.

━ ━

"I didn't know where to go," I said, standing at the doorstep.

It was around eleven o'clock at night, and the weather was bad. I was drenched from head to toe for waiting for a bus in the rain and snow. I had no place to go after my breakup from De'Andre.

"Yo Pierre, come in."

I strode into the huge foyer, dripping on the white marble floors. The house was dark, as if everyone had retired to bed early. My shoes squeaked as I turned around, facing Vijay as he closed the door with a soft click. He took my bags and led me into the kitchen. He switched on the recess lights and asked me if I would like anything to drink. I was going to say wine, but I remembered his family didn't drink, so I asked for water. I looked around the kitchen. It seemed as if I'd stepped into Martha Stewart's home. The kitchen was all white, with see-through glass cabinets hosting ceramic white plates and cups. Jay handed me a glass of water and took a seat next to me at the granite island counter.

"Thanks for replying to my text," I said.

"No prob, man. So, what happened?"

"I broke off the engagement with Dre."

"Woah."

"Yeah, I know."

"How come?" he asked, still in shock.

"He got his intern pregnant."

"How do you know this?"

"She dropped by my place while Dre was out. She came over because Dre wasn't responding to her texts. He even blackmailed her by saying if she told me or anyone about the pregnancy, he would terminate her at the CBC."

"How do you know this thot isn't lying?"

"She showed me the pregnancy results that she and Dre took at Sunnybrook Hospital. The DNA matched."

"Wow, Pierre. You two been together for a long time."

"I know."

CONFUSED SPICE

"What are you going to do now?"

"I have no idea. I guess find a place of my own. I still have the OMNI gig to look forward to."

"I hate to tell you, Pierre, but living in this city is ridiculously expensive."

"Well, there's always the option to move back to Detroit."

"Do you have money?"

"Yes, I have enough to get me by a few months."

"Well ... if you ever need some money, let me know. I can always postpone my trip to India." Vijay's dark eyes were pressing on me. Now I felt like shit. When Vijay was going through his hard times paying his rent and moving out, I didn't help at all. Some great friend I was.

"Thanks, Vijay. I really appreciate it."

"No problem."

"Are you sure your parents wouldn't mind me staying here tonight?"

Vijay fell silent for a moment. "Not at all, man, they will be fine. Besides, you're my guest."

Jay showed me to the guest room on the second floor. The room was spacious, with its own bathroom and walk-in closet. I sat my bags on the bed and turned to Vijay, who regarded me from the doorway. He told me his room was just next door, and if I needed anything, just holla.

After he left, I lay across the king-size bed with my hands locked behind my head, reflecting on the day. My relationship with De'Andre was over. I couldn't believe it. I would be lying to say I didn't miss him already. But I knew I couldn't continue to let him mistreat me the way he had been doing. It was unacceptable. However, in the back of mind I wondered if I'd made the right decision leaving him and coming here.

241

MATHIS BAILEY

I couldn't believe I was in Vijay's house. The house he grew up in. I turned on my side in the bed facing the window watching the lightning light up the room. What the hell was I going to do back in Detroit? I guessed I'd have to live with my parents until I found a place of my own. I could go back into nursing. I felt ashamed; I was thirty and still didn't know the purpose of my life. I turned over and closed my eyes and listened to the rain tap on the window.

—— ——

The next morning, I was awakened by the smell of fried turkey bacon. I opened my eyes to find the room filled with sunlight. At first, I was disoriented, not knowing where I was. I reached for my phone and saw I had one missed call from Dre. Last night seemed as if it was a nightmare. I still couldn't grasp the fact that our relationship had met its demise, and I was now here at Vijay's parents' semi-mansion. I climbed out of the fluffy sheets, went to the adjacent bathroom, and splashed water onto my face. I then went to Vijay's room next to mine. When I entered, he was doing pushups while listening to music wearing earbuds. Sunlight came through his window and painted his shirtless body the color of amber beer. I walked into his room, closing the door behind me. The click of the door caused him to look up.

"Did you sleep well?" he asked, standing up covered with a thin layer of sweat.

"Yes. I did."

"That's good," he said, taking the white buds out of his ears.

"I can't believe you're wearing those."

"What?" He scrunched his brows.

242

CONFUSED SPICE

"Earphones."

"Oh." He laughed.

"I'm used to you always blasting your music," I said.

"I know, my parents hate that shit yo. Hey! Are you hungry?"

"Yeah, famished."

As we made our way to the kitchen, his mother and stepfather were sitting at the island counter enjoying their morning breakfast. Mrs. Morrison chewed on her toast as she typed away on her laptop with her reading glasses perched on the edge of her petite nose. She slowly looked up at me as we strolled into the kitchen. Mr. Morrison was too busy with his face buried into the *Toronto Star* newspaper to notice us. Mrs. Morrison rose from her half-eaten breakfast and placed a hand on her husband's back. He slowly brought the paper down from his face.

"Vijay, may I see you in the study?" asked Mrs. Morrison.

"Yeah, but let me first make my guest breakfast."

"Good morning, Mr. and Mrs. Morrison. Sorry for the imposition but..."

"You don't need to explain, Pierre. You're my guest."

"And this is my house," said Mrs. Morrison. "Vijay, you cannot just bring anyone off the streets into our home."

"He isn't just anyone, he's my friend," Vijay retorted.

"Vijay, you should have consulted with us that you were having a guest staying over at our home," said Frank.

"I know, but it was short notice. Pierre needed a place to bunk just for the night."

Mrs. Morrison stepped forward. "I don't want your hooligan friends staying in this house. There's no telling what trouble they will bring here. Think about your little sister and grandmother. Vijay, you need to think before you do. What about my representation? You know I'm always in the public eye. I can't afford to

243

have those damn reporters knocking on my door snooping in my personal affairs, especially that De'Andre Harris." She looked at me as if to remind me of her threat.

I looked at Jay and said, "I think I should go,"

"Yes, perhaps you should," said Mrs. Morrison, advancing as I made my way toward the stairs to gather my things. After I collected my bags from the room, Jay took me to a café around the corner from his parent's home to grab a bite to eat.

After we chose a table, Vijay brought back two piping hot cups of coffee, two buttered croissants, and a mixed bowl of fruit. He still looked upset about what transpired at his parents' place, but I felt like it was my fault. Yet I sensed that Vijay had known this time was coming. I picked up my cup and took a sip as Vijay spoke.

"Why don't you come to India with me?" The sudden question almost made me spit out my coffee.

"Are you serious?"

"Yeah, *son*," he said in his pretend New York accent. "We will have fun."

I thought about it for a moment. For sure it was a crazy idea, but that was what I liked about Vijay; he was unpredictable. I thought about the OMNI job. I would see if I could get an extension on a start date. I thought about the price of the ticket. I had a little bit of money saved, but the trip alone probably would wipe me clean. And then what? I couldn't go back to my parents' place jobless and flat broke.

"I don't know, Vijay, I mean, I don't think I can afford such a trip."

"Yo, don't worry about the cost."

"Vijay, NO!" I exclaimed. "I'm not letting you pay for me."

CONFUSED SPICE

"Who said anything about me paying for you?" he said, biting into his croissant with a smirk.

"Oh." I felt chagrined.

"I have a buddy that works for Air Canada. I can have him hook us up with a decent discount, hotel included."

"Fa-real?" I said in my typical Detroit accent.

"Yeah, how do you think I was paying for my trip? Certainly not from bussing tables."

"Well ... I thought your parents were..."

"Man, please..." he said, cutting me off. "I stopped asking them for money. So are you coming?"

"Jay, I don't know ... this is crazy... How will we get around? We don't know a thing about India, and we certainly don't speak Hindi."

Vijay took a swift sip of his coffee. "That's the thrilling part of it."

"Jay, you love living on the edge." I laughed.

He grinned and said, "Yes *siiirr*. This is going to be an amazing trip, Pierre Jackson. Trust me. I need this change, and so do you."

"But Vijay, what about your mother?"

"What about her?"

"I don't understand why she despises me so much."

He took another sip of his coffee before answering. "She sees me in you."

"What?"

"It doesn't matter, man."

"No. Tell me," I pressed.

"I'll tell you later, Pierre, but now lets make these reservations," he said.

245

After we finished our breakfast, Vijay called his buddy who worked at the airline and booked another ticket for India. Everything was set and done. I wondered where my feelings lay with Vijay. They were all tangled up. One minute he was driving me up the wall, and the next he was making me feel butterflies in my stomach, which I'd never experienced before, not even with Dre.

31

Pierre

An hour later we arrived at the Marriott Hotel near Pearson airport.

The room was modest with one bed, a sofa, a few modern paintings hanging along the walls, and a mini refrigerator tucked in the corner. Jay and I left our luggage near the door. I couldn't believe within the next couple of days we would be in Lonavla, India. Vijay's spiritual buddies had recommended this meditation retreat at a place called The Machaan. It's a remote village on a hill. It's supposed to have a spa, an infinity pool, a beautiful wildlife, and a twenty-four-hour meditation and yoga class, food included. Now I had a reason to become vegetarian. This trip would do Jay and I some good. But before arriving in Lonavla, Jay wanted to stop in Mumbai to find his father. He'd told me about his mother's past, and I felt sorry for him and for her on what she'd been through. His grandmother had given him the address where his father might be staying. I think it was a good thing for Vijay to actually speak with his father. Perhaps it would help him move forward with his life.

"Are you going to continue to look for your father if he isn't at that address?" I asked.

"Maybe," he said, taking a swig from his beer that he'd unearthed from the mini fridge.

"Do you think he will recognize you?"

He strode to the window and watched the planes take off in the far distance.

"He may recognize me, but I have no idea. I just hope he's chilled the fuck out over the years."

"I'm sure he will have," I managed to say optimistically. He turned around and looked at me and leaned against the window ledge with his ankles crossed as if he was a carbon copy of James Dean. His dark eyebrows sat heavy on his beautiful espresso-colored face. His hair was lined up and cut close, giving him much swag. I felt the butterflies in my stomach coming alive. Why did he stare at me this way? *Shit!*

"That's what I like about you, Pierre. You always think on the positive side. You are so good for me." He strolled toward me and took up residency beside me on the bed, disturbing the smoothness of the white sheet on his side. He was so close that I could smell the essence of the coconut oil in his hair, mingling with the caramel, malty scent from his breath.

"I'm glad you've feel that way, Jay." I smiled.

"Do you miss him?"

"Who?"

"Dre."

CONFUSED SPICE

"Oh, a little," I said. There were moments I felt like calling him, but I knew it would be foolish to do so. It felt strange waking up with him not next to me or holding me close in bed. But I couldn't turn back now. I had come so far. Vijay looked down at the frayed carpet and then back up at me as if reading my thoughts.

"You deserve better," he said matter-of-factly.

"I know," I breathed. I could sense that confused space arising between us like an inflated balloon. I tried to think of something quickly to say without things getting awkward. "How are you going to go about looking for your father if that address doesn't work?"

"Well, I know his name, Joshi Khakwani. I guess I could ask his old neighbors or the locals regarding his whereabouts. They should know. I've heard India is like a big family. Everyone knows each other."

"Well ... I hope we find him in over a billion people."

He stuck out his bottom lip in that shrewd way. "Well, I will figure out plan C when we get there." He smirked and took another swig of his cold beer.

When Jay left the room to work out in the hotel's gym, I made a few phone calls. I sat on the bed and dug in my pocket for my phone to dial my mother's number to let her know what happened between Dre and me. After a couple rings, she picked up. She was sorry to hear what had happened but probably knew it was for the best. I could hear in her soothing voice that she was proud of me, probably for doing something that she hadn't had the courage to do in her marriage. But I was proud of her for making her marriage work. After I got off the phone with her, I called my job at Saks Fifth Avenue to see if my boss had received

249

MATHIS BAILEY

my resignation that I'd emailed a week ago upon getting a job at OMNI. My last day there was tomorrow, but I asked one of my coworkers to cover my last shift.

After I got a confirmation from my boss that it had been received, the next person I called was Dre. There was an awkward silence on the phone. He asked me if I was safe and okay. I said yes. To cut to the chase, I had told him about Mrs. Morrison's potentially exposing his affair. He instantly knew who she was from hearing her name in the news, winning cases for politicians. However, he didn't know she was Vijay's mother. He asked me if I was the one who had told her about his affair. When I didn't answer, he knew I wouldn't stoop that low. I was mad at him for what he did, but I wouldn't do anything to jeopardize his career. Then it dawned on us that the culprit could be his intern, who probably sought out Mrs. Morrison to represent her in court if Dre refused to pay child support. Dre fell silent, probably wondering how he had gotten himself into such a mess: getting an intern pregnant, destroying his relationship with me, and potentially losing his job. But I told him everything would be alright. He asked how. I told him about Mrs. Morrison's secret. Her leaving India. Another long silence followed, and I could tell I gave him a glimmer of hope. I was pretty sure he would get to her before she got to him. He probably would blackmail her in an email the next day, giving her a taste of her own medicine. All of a sudden our voices were mellow and low. Deep down, he knew I wasn't coming back, and there was nothing he could do or say to change my mind.

CONFUSED SPICE

It was a sun-soaked Monday morning when we arrived at the airport. Vijay parked his black Acura in the storage parking lot free of charge thanks to his friend. We strode into the United Emirates terminal and stood in line. We stood behind an Indian woman wearing a green and red sari with white running shoes. Her hair was smoothly swept back and parted neatly in the middle. She stood with a little girl who held tight to her leg. The woman had four huge suitcases wrapped with duct tape with red ribbons hanging from them. I wondered how she managed to carry all of it by herself.

Once Vijay and I made it to the counter, a beautiful woman wearing red lipstick and a beige cap with a thin white scarf around her neck weighed our bags and sent them on a conveyor belt and gave us our tickets.

After we went through the metal detectors, we had another hour to kill before our flight took off. We located our terminal and looked around for a place to sit and have lunch. We strode pass a couple of eateries that looked pretty decent. The airport was huge. This was my first time inside Pearson. People sat in chairs reading paperback novels, some sleeping with their legs hiked up on their luggage as they waited for their flight to be called. We found a pub-looking café not too far away from our terminal.

"I can't believe we are actually doing this," I said after we placed in our order on an electronic menu tablet.

"Believe it, Pierre," he said with a grin.

"Have your parents tried contacting you since you left?"

"Nope."

"Are you serious?"

"Yeah, but that's okay."

251

MATHIS BAILEY

"They will come around," I said, not quite sure why his parents were so against him going to India. Seeing his father couldn't be all it. I knew his mother wanted him to finish school; perhaps that was it. Besides, we were only going for three weeks, not a year. We were, after all, talking about Vijay Khakwani, who liked to change his mind at the last minute.

I thought about our conversation last night in the hotel. He had told me there was something he had to tell me once we were in India. What could it possibly be?

Jay looked down at his watch and said they would be boarding shortly. We finished up our pastrami sandwiches and headed toward our terminal.

When we boarded the aircraft, I located our seats while Vijay placed our carry-ons in the upper compartment. I sat near the window and looked out at the black tarmac. *Within twenty-four hours, I will be in India!* my inner voice screamed. It's so strange how life deals out its hand. I heard the plane door shut. I looked over at Vijay, who pulled a spiritual book from his traveling backpack. The plane jolted and started to move.

"This is going to be an amazing trip. Trust me yo."

I smiled and sank back into my seat, gazing out of the window with the sun's rays glowing on my face. I had no idea what to expect once we landed in India. I knew whatever happened, I would be with a person who wouldn't let anything bad happen to me. I felt safe with Vijay, and I was sure he felt the same with me. I didn't know where we would end up in our strange relationship. But I did know I liked the space that we were in; that space that has no limits, the space that seems boundless, and the space that seems to be infused with pure bliss. I finally felt as if I was headed toward happiness in my life. It's strange how life comes at you in ways that you least expect. I wondered if there was a special

CONFUSED SPICE

place in Vijay's heart for me. But I wouldn't think about that now.
I would enjoy just being.

A beautiful flight attendant strode down the aisle pushing
a silver cart offering drinks. I got a ginger ale while Vijay got a
cup of herbal tea. He sipped it and leaned back in his chair as
if he was ready to doze off. He turned toward me, staring out
the window at the hazy sunset that painted the sky orange and
a blush red. He smiled and drifted off to sleep. I reclined my
chair, aligning with his, just inches away from his sun-soaked
face. I stared at him for a moment before closing my eyes and
experiencing supreme space.

Epilogue

Vijay

It was an early morning when I stopped by to see Dr. McKenzie. I decided to pay a visit before I took off for India. I ran a hand over my face and darted my eyes around the spacious room to the various degrees hanging along the walls. My cup of green tea sitting on the coffee table probably had grown cold since it was given to me fifteen minutes ago. I thought to get up and pour some more from the electric pot, since the doc was too immersed in my fuckin' life. But I was too relaxed to move lying across the sofa.

"I already decided, Doc. I'm going to India."

"For what?"

"To look for my father and perhaps to become a monk."

"Are you ready to meet him?"

MATHIS BAILEY

"Kinda. I can't say I'm not nervous. He probably moved on and started a new life, remarried, and had more kids."

"How does your mother feel about you looking for your biological father?"

"Not too thrilled yo. She's probably afraid that he might come back into her life and do some harm. But I don't think that's going to happen. It's not like I'm going over there to talk about her new life to him. Her personal life is her business. I just want to meet the man whose blood runs through my veins. The man whose ancestry I share. My mother shouldn't worry. I got this thing under control."

"Well, it sounds like you are making some progress, Vijay. I think seeing your father will do you some good, emotionally and mentally. Perhaps close some old wounds you may harbor."

"I'm not harboring anything, Doc," I said, taking offense.

The doc adjusted his glasses on his nose and spoke again. "What about Pierre?"

"What about him?" I said sharply.

"Where do you two stand in your relationship?"

This fucking question always made me pause. I looked at the doc, and he peered back at me over his glasses like a studious English professor overseeing a quiet class during a NO-TALKING exam. I glanced up at the black-and-white digital clock mounted on the wall, seconds were ticking away. I noticed I had a few minutes left before my time was up. I imagined Pierre back at the hotel sleeping in the white sheets. We'd slept in the same bed last night after I experienced some rough nights on the stiff sofa in our room. Pierre insisted I sleep in the bed since there was more than enough room for two people. I woke up this morning with a fucking hard-on. My dick bounced with

256

CONFUSED SPICE

every indecent thought that ran rapidly in my mind as I stared at Pierre sleeping on his stomach with his ass facing up in those tight pajama bottoms. Before I did anything I might regret, I got up, strolled into the bathroom, and took a cold shower to relax my tense muscles. I got dressed and decided to see my doc one last time. I ripped a piece of paper from the hotel's notepad and wrote a message to Pierre telling him I had stepped out and would be back before our 11:45 a.m. flight. I left the note on the side table next to him.

I looked at the doc and said, "I don't know where we stand."

"What do you mean?"

"Like I fuckin' said ... I don't know. Pierre is the first dude I ever felt this close to. He's more than a friend, more than a brother. I can't place him in a box, if that makes any sense yo."

"What will happen to your friendship with Pierre once you go to India?"

I glanced at the doc and said, "I asked him to come along."

"And he agreed?"

"Yeah. He is going through a tough break-up with his fiancé. And to take his mind off it, I invited him along to India. I think it will do him some good."

The doc shifted in his chair, cleared his throat, placed his yellow pad on the coffee table in front of him, and rose. My eyes followed him to his desk and watched him pour himself a cup of tea. Steam wisped into the air as he took a sip and leaned against his desk. He ran his fingers through his thinning gray hair before speaking again.

"Vijay, your time is up."

257

Acknowledgements

I would like to give special thanks to Reema Jaffer, Patricia Lezcano, Rena Scott and Kailee Fatt for being my beta readers. I really appreciated the feedback. Thanks to my editor, Allister Thompson, for making this story even better. A tremendous thanks to my graphic designer, Daniel Cullen, for his incredible patience and creating a beautiful cover. You really saw my vision. Last but not least, my family and friends. I couldn't have made it this far without your love and support. Thank you.

Feel free to stop by www.mathisbailey.com

Recipes

MY FAMOUS KEEMA
Serves 4

1 pound of ground lamb	1 teaspoon salt
1 onion chopped	1 teaspoon pepper
1 teaspoon minced garlic	½ cup green peas
1 teaspoon minced ginger	½ cup mild harissa sauce (recommend Mina brand)
1 teaspoon garam masala	1 cinnamon stick
½ teaspoon chili powder	3 cups of water

Place ground lamb in a stainless-steel bowl with two cups of water. Stir vigorously with a fork for 1 minute until the mixture becomes lump free. Set aside.

Sautee the onions with oil in a skillet on mid-high heat. Add minced garlic and ginger. Stir for a minute and then add garam masala, chili powder, salt and pepper. Stir for a few seconds, and add the ground lamb mixture, stirring continuously until lightly brown. Add harissa sauce, green peas and cinnamon stick. Add 1 cup of water. Cover, and let simmer for 20-25 minutes.

Serve with basmati rice or naan.

SPICY SOUTHWESTERN TACO PIE
Serves 8

1-pound lean ground chicken	19-ounce can black beans, drained
1 onion	11-ounce can whole corn, drained
1 Jalapeno (deseeded and diced)	2 cups sharp cheddar cheese
1 pack hot taco Seasoning	½ cup salsa

1 teaspoon minced garlic
1 teaspoon pepper
1 15-ounce package
refrigerated pie crust

½ cup sour cream

Sautee onions and jalapeno with oil in a skillet until translucent on mid high heat. Stir in garlic and then ground chicken. Cook for 5 minutes. Stir in taco seasoning and pepper. Cook for 1 minute. Add corn, black beans and salsa. Stir until mixture is combined. Set aside.

Unroll one pie dough and place it in a non-stick pie dish. Place one layer of meat mixture at the bottom, then one cup of cheddar cheese on top. Repeat this process. Place the last pie dough on top. Pinch the edges to lock in moisture.

Preheat Oven on 350. Bake for 30 minutes until golden brown.

Take out oven and set to cool for 15 minutes.

Garnish with a dollop of sour cream.

THREE LAYER MOIST RED VELVET CAKE
Serves 12

2 cups flour
1 teaspoon baking soda
1 teaspoon cocoa
1 ½ cups granulated sugar
2 eggs

1 cup vegetable oil
1 teaspoon vinegar

1-ounce red food coloring

1 cup buttermilk

butter cream icing
1 ½ powder sugar
2 teaspoons bourbon vanilla extract
1 cup chopped pecans
1 stick salted butter, room temperature
2 boxes cream cheese, room temperature

MATHIS BAILEY

2 teaspoons bourbon
vanilla extract

Preheat oven 350

Take a big stainless-steel bowl and combine vegetable oil,
buttermilk, granulated sugar, eggs and vanilla extract. Mix well
with an electric mixer for 1 minute. Add flour, baking soda, cocoa powder, red food coloring and vinegar. Mix for 1 minute
until smooth. Set aside

Brush three small non-stick baking pans with oil, and then
dust inside lightly with flour. Pour cake batter evenly into pans.
Bake for 8-10 minutes. Once done, set aside to cool.

Meanwhile, take a stainless-steel bowl combine powder sugar, cream cheese, vanilla extract and butter. Mix well with an
electric mix for 1 minute until smooth.

Ice the top of the cakes with an icing knife. Then stack them
evenly on top of each other. Once done, ice the sides.

Garnish with chopped pecans on top.

Made in the USA
Charleston, SC
11 January 2017